D1475094

Managing
in the
Corporate Interest

Managing in the Corporate Interest

*Control and Resistance
in an American Bank*

HG
1615
.S64
1990
west

Vicki Smith

UNIVERSITY OF CALIFORNIA PRESS
BERKELEY LOS ANGELES OXFORD

University of California Press
Berkeley and Los Angeles, California

University of California Press, Ltd.
Oxford, England

© 1990 by
The Regents of the University of California

Library of Congress Cataloging-in-Publication Data

Smith, Vicki, 1951–
    Managing in the corporate interest : control and resistance in an
American bank / Vicki Smith
        p. cm.
    Includes bibliographical references.
    ISBN 0–520–06779–7 (alk. paper)
    1. Bank management–United States. 2. Middle managers–United
States. I. Title.
HG1615.S64 1990
332.1'068—dc20   90–10780

Printed in the United States of America
1 2 3 4 5 6 7 8 9

The paper used in this publication meets the minimum requirements of
American National Standard for Information Sciences—Permanence of
Paper for Printed Library Materials, ANSI Z39.48-1984. ∞™

To my family

Contents

Acknowledgments

Over the years several mentors and friends made this research and writing possible. I was fortunate enough to work with two of the very best faculty members in the University of California, Berkeley, Department of Sociology, where I began studying American Security Bank as a dissertation project. Working with Michael Burawoy on this project was always a delight and a challenge—or perhaps I should say it was a challenge and a delight. I continually learned from his critical and constructive comments. As my dissertation adviser, his guidance of and enthusiasm for my research project were invaluable. His commitment to critical thinking and to his students stands as an exemplary academic model.

Arlie Hochschild supported every stage of my dissertation project and pushed me to rethink both preliminary conceptions of my research and the process of writing itself.

In an ongoing dissertation group, Linda Blum, Louise Jezierski, and Brian Powers provided absolutely vital reassurance and feedback about writing and doing research. I continue to benefit from their friendship.

Likewise Bob Freeland, Linda Fuller, Karen Hansen, Greg McLauchlan, and Jennifer Pierce continually lent their personal and intellectual support during and beyond the thesis-writing process. Robin Leidner, Fred Block, and Michael Useem kindly gave me valuable comments on the arguments and data in this manuscript.

Although this book will be published long after her untimely death, I would nevertheless like to thank Carol Hatch for the supportive role she played in my graduate studies. Politically and intellectually she was a mainstay for many graduate students and for the Department of Sociology at Berkeley. Without a doubt, she deserves at least a few grateful acknowledgments in the many books written by students and faculty from Berkeley.

My family was always unwavering in their assistance: Helen Smith, Diana Smith, Susan and Lewis Brockus, Brian McMahon, June and Mark McMahon, and Constance and David Claghorn strongly encouraged me throughout this project. While I was revising this manuscript, Bob Larchwood's antics saved me from many a tedious day.

Steve McMahon's intellectual, emotional, and moral encouragement helped me genuinely to appreciate the rewarding aspects of writing and to weather the discouraging aspects with the highest degree of integrity that one could expect. Many of the ideas of this book developed as a result of long, often heated discussions about its central claims. On various occasions he helped me see the forest through the trees, something especially difficult with the complex and mountainous data collected in field work. The process and product would have been very different without him.

1

Social Change and the Study of Management

It is impossible to speak of the premier role of the American corporation in the world economy without speaking of American management systems. Institutionalized and professionalized when the large corporation gained hold after World War II, the American management system has been trusted and admired by the national and international business community. Indeed, many believe that American corporate management was responsible for the dominant economic position held by the United States in the postwar period.

But just as that dominant corporate role has been severely shaken over the past two decades, so too has the function of management itself. U.S. corporations have struggled to maintain profitability, restructuring themselves organizationally to survive in a globally competitive era. And in an unprecedented fashion, corporate leaders and management experts have attacked middle management for its role in blocking and even actively undermining these corporate survival strategies. Middle management became in the 1980s what labor was in the 1970s: a convenient scapegoat for economic decline. While business leaders furiously disinvested, merged, acquired, and "downsized" business operations, they frequently used a stinging critique of middle management to justify these actions.

Others now question the future of middle management in U.S. business because of the growing perception that strict hierarchies have a debilitating effect on the corporation and that empowered workers can play a positive and productive role in new systems of working and producing. As never before, business researchers and observers, industrial relations experts, and managers themselves are reflecting on corporate authority relations, asking hard questions about the institutional reinforcements of traditional hierarchies and privileges and debating whether these historically constructed relationships should endure.

Clear linkages exist between the restructuring of corporations to regain competitiveness and the fundamental critique of American management. Yet social scientists and the millions of people who work in our largest corporations lack systematic sociological evidence about the relationship between the two. The implications of corporate and managerial change are largely delimited by descriptive accounts in the press, popular management books that obscure structural changes in the organization of management work, and a managerial literature that diagnoses the human costs of corporate restructuring as inevitable "human resources predicaments," taking for granted business leaders' mission to "downsize" the American corporation.[1]

1. Although they cannot be the sole basis for generating sociological findings, any one of these sources provides secondary forms of data that support sociological field research on managerial and organizational transformations. For example, business publications are excellent sources of information about corporate change, and in some cases the only sources. They report personnel and organizational restructuring policies so recently implemented that findings pertaining to them have not yet entered into the academic literature. I draw on several of the most reliable business publications (the *Wall Street Journal, New York Times, Businessweek*) to suggest the prevalence of certain phenomena, as well as the possible generalizability of claims made in this study. Likewise, despite its administrative bias, much human resources literature provides useful data about conflict and

Drawing on an in-depth case study, this book analyzes the consequences of industrial restructuring for American middle management.[2] Why study middle management? One answer is empirical: despite extensive commentary on the changing face of corporate life, we know little about the transformation of power, authority relations, and work of middle managers. This book asks whether retrenchment and restructuring transform managerial work processes and the division of labor between managerial and nonmanagerial employees. It also investigates the political processes caused by restructuring. How do middle managers respond to change and how can we explain those responses?

The limited scholarly data available on this topic come from researchers studying organizational decline, who have only just begun to analyze the consequences of restructuring for middle managers. The decline perspective argues that the new competitive environment (scarcer resources, shrinking markets) forces organizational leaders to take the unavoidable steps of downgrading and scaling back operations. In turn, these researchers nearly unanimously claim (Whetton 1988), restructuring and retrenchment create "dysfunctional" dynamics that top-level organization leaders must manage. Lower-level managers, for example, subsequently respond to decline with denial (Krantz 1988); conflict, secrecy, scapegoating (Cameron, Kim, and Whetton 1987); avoidance of innovation (Whetton 1988); concealment behind psychological and organizational "exit barriers" (Harrigan 1988); and other con-

---

consent in the context of, and the organizational practices associated with, corporate restructuring processes. And, of course, popular management books are a gauge of new trends in management. All three sources can also yield hypotheses for work on this little-explored topic.

2. The term "industrial restructuring" refers not only to the restructuring of traditional, narrowly defined industrial concerns (such as manufacturing and heavy industry) but also to the restructuring of all industries, sectors composed of similar firms in manufacturing, service, transportation, and so on. For one discussion of industrial restructuring see Henderson and Castells (1987); see Useem (1989) for a discussion of corporate restructuring.

servative and irrational resistance strategies that top managers must overcome.

The decline literature, however, fails to question the stand-
point from which rational action is defined or the politics
involved in defining rational behavior. They assume that
current restructuring policies are inevitable and that only organization *leaders* can define the best interests of the corporate organization, as well as the appropriate actions for
achieving those interests. Like earlier research on bureaucracies that identifies different logics of rational action within
the organization (Blau 1955; Crozier 1964; Gouldner 1954),
the research presented here empirically investigates and crit-
icizes this one-sided conception of rational action, corporate
interests, and organizational change. Unlike those earlier
studies, which tended to focus solely on internal organizational forces, this study also analyzes managerial action in
relation to external structural, cultural, and economic forces;
specifically, it links managerial action to macro-level changes
in the political economy.

A second reason for this study is analytic: middle managers have a pivotal and contradictory role in corporate restructuring processes. More to the point, middle management
may be at the center of industrial restructuring. This book
explores that role, using one case study to understand the
processes that have fundamentally reshaped American middle
management in the 1980s. On the one hand, a constant stream
of reports and studies suggests a significant and unprecedented decline in the employment conditions and status of
middle levels of management in large, historically oligopolistic firms. On the other, we live in an era that devotes considerable attention to the critical role middle managers play in
improving American industrial competitiveness. Insofar as
these two tendencies appear as separate processes, they seem
extremely contradictory. Yet they actually reflect the same
process: an agenda for transforming the function of management by targeting corporate middle managers simulta-

neously as objects and agents of corporate decline and reconstruction.

This study portrays middle managers in the transition to a new competitive era. It documents the attempts of the top managers of a large, traditionally paternalistic banking firm to position middle managers as objects and agents of corporate restructuring. Specifically, it shows how top management transformed the traditional organizational bases of managerial authority while relying on middle managers to legitimate and accelerate a downsizing process. By examining the degradation of the managerial position at the heart of one major corporate transformation, as well as the intramanagement politics of degradation, the study demonstrates the struggle over who will take what responsibility for restructuring American corporations. After summarizing, in the next section, the numerous and diverse indicators of fundamental change in the work, organization, and ideology of management, I briefly discuss the in-depth case I use to analyze these changes and then summarize the overall argument of the book.

Restructuring Management and Managing Restructuring

Proposals for new ways of organizing work and management have acquired an urgent tone in the wake of two decades of corporate restructuring. Since the late 1960s the American political economy has faced many challenges to its international dominance; by now most commentators agree that the United States has entered a qualitatively new and different era of economic competition.

Many agree that the increasingly competitive pressures of the late 1960s and the 1970s triggered this transition. Profitability crises resulting from greater international competition, contracting markets, and deregulation caused significant plant mobility and closures, job loss, high merger and acquisition activity, and disinvestment of productive capac-

ity (Bluestone and Harrison 1982; Bowles, Gordon, and
Weisskopf 1984; LeGrande 1983; Corrigan and Stanfield 1984;
Fallows 1985; Wallace and Rothschild 1988). Furthermore, in
the absence of real and sustained economic growth, top U.S.
corporate management decreased its investment in productive activity and enterprises, instead promoting the illusion
of prosperity in a form of profit gains on paper—what Reich
(1983) calls "paper entrepreneurialism" and Bluestone and
Harrison (1982) call "new managerialism": the "thoroughly
legal, aboveboard conglomerate strategies . . . that emphasize cash management over a commitment to any particular
product line" (p. 150). Disinvestment, mergers, and acquisitions—the principal means of building assets on paper—are
driving forces behind job loss, corporate recentralization,
technological unemployment, and regional shifts of industry.[3]

The devastation inflicted on manufacturing and other blue-
collar workers as a result of these processes has been
extensively studied, but the unprecedented, often dire
consequences for managerial workers are less well known.
Bluestone and Harrison (1982), for example, suggest that
disinvestment and deindustrialization "unemployed" large
numbers of managerial and other workers. Professional and
managerial workers experienced the greatest downward mobility of the displaced workers they studied (p. 55), indicating
that deindustrialization reconfigures the managerial as well
as the manufacturing portion of the American occupational
structure. In other words, managers were not immune from
the displacement processes affecting workers.

A study of the reemployment outcomes for 5 million workers displaced by plant closures, layoffs, and cutbacks between
1979 and 1984 provides further evidence that industrial
changes adversely affect managers. Among the 3.1 million

---

3. See also Hardy and Pettigrew (1985), Munro (1985), Sheinkman (1985), Staudohar and Brown (1987, part 3), who analyze top
management's role in facilitating corporate restructuring.

workers who were reemployed by January 1984, 525,000 were in managerial and professional occupations in their previous job. Only one-half were reemployed in such jobs, however, a reintegration rate similar, for example, to that of precision production, craft, and repair workers (Flaim and Sehgal 1987, table 9-13).

Increased international competition has wreaked havoc on historically secure corporations and their strategies to achieve profitability. Firms across a spectrum of activities and locations abruptly changed their product market orientations and subjected employees across the board to radical alterations of organizational structure and employment conditions. Corporate leaders streamlined their firms to become more competitive and profitable; in basic manufacturing, telecommunications, and financial services industries, top managers aggressively attacked their corporate staffs and operations managers in the effort to reduce administrative overhead. Indeed, it seems that the decline and restructuring processes affecting managers, as well as other workers, knew few market or sectoral bounds in the economic climate of the 1980s (Cameron, Sutton, and Whetton 1988, introduction). Even in so-called growth industries, major firms responded to greater competition by paring down corporate size and centralizing functions (*Wall Street Journal*, 26 October 1984).

Popular and euphemistic notions of "flattening the organizational hierarchy" or "removing layers of bureaucracy" aided the streamlining process. Corporate top managements, committed to doing away with overly bureaucratized systems, slashed away at middle managerial jobs, reducing overhead and the number of layers through which communications and decision making travel.[4] No one mentions what

4. See, for example, the unmitigated enthusiasm for paring down the corporate hierarchy in a *New York Times* feature: noted author and management consultant Tom Peters (1985), listing British Steel's cut of corporate staff from 1,000 to 175, Dana Corporation's cut from 600 to 85 corporate members and from fifteen to five layers of management, and the Brunswick Corporation's cut from 600 to 200 cor-

"paring down" means for managers who once occupied the abstract "layers of bureaucracy" or, indeed, what eliminating management levels means for those remaining in the corporation. But without a doubt American business has become firmly committed to cutting the administrative layers staffed principally by middle management (Osterman 1988, p. 81). By removing the intervening levels of bureaucratic management that characterized the large, growth-oriented corporation of the post–World War II era, these efforts additionally allow top managements to regain and maximize control over production processes.[5]

Corporate mergers and takeovers adversely affected middle management.[6] Although middle managers might have been retained to ensure the success of newly merged corporations, mergers more frequently caused managerial redundancy. New executives and boards of directors phased out entire divisions or functions and often dropped particular jobs or selected managers (*New York Times*, 17 October 1982a; Hartman and Hill 1983).[7] Managerial and nonmanagerial personnel both

---

porate staff members, cites increased profitability, productivity, and management effectiveness as direct outcomes. Such examples abound in the pages of the *Wall Street Journal*, the *New York Times*, and major business and management publications.

5. New flexible manufacturing technologies, such as CAD/CAM (Computer-Aided Design/Computer-Aided Management), have also led to the elimination of levels of middle management. Helfgott (1988) goes so far as to claim that flexible technology has affected the structure of *management* in the enterprise far more profoundly than it has affected the work of blue-collar employees. I do not discuss technology in depth in this section because I wish to focus on the direct external macroeconomic and cultural forces that have been reshaping middle management in the last decade.

6. Mergers, acquisitions, and divestitures of over $1 million increased 233 percent in the ten years between 1977 and 1986 (1,209 in 1977 to 4,024 in 1986) ("Ten-Year Merger Completion Record," 1987, p. 57). The numbers dropped over the next two years (3,920 in 1987; 3,487 in 1988) ("1988 Profile," 1989, p. 53); nevertheless the activity is still fairly high-pitched.

7. See Ravenscroft and Scherer (1987) for an enlightening discussion of the difficulties that "merger makers" encounter in control-

ended up paying, with their jobs or wage cuts, for the financial debt accumulated in the course of leveraged buyouts and takeovers. But management experts report that corporate raiders often first cut layers of management in order to raise cash, enhance shareholder value, and gain greater control over the firm. The estimates of the number of jobs cut in this process vary. Some claim that merger and acquisition activity forced nearly half a million "executive, administrative, and managerial" workers out of their jobs between 1981 and 1986 (Willis 1987; *Fortune*, 2 March 1987), while others speculate that more than two million corporate managers lost their jobs in the 1980s as a result of restructuring (*New York Times*, 24 January 1988).[8]

Deregulation, mergers, and acquisitions, and subsequent struggles for industrial competitiveness, can slow promotion rates for middle managers (as opportunities for upward mobility decrease, middle managers are stalled at position plateaus) (Hall and Isabella 1985; Hodgetts, Lawrence, and Schlesinger 1985), while cutbacks in vertical integration (or "disaggregation," in which firms shed all but core productive activities) lead to the excision of layers of management (Thackray 1986).

---

ling and integrating the management structures of companies they acquire.

8. Such estimates must be taken with caution. According to the Bureau of Labor Statistics, the precise numbers of managerial, professional, and administrative employees displaced by mergers and acquisitions have not been systematically tracked. Where there are estimates, it can be difficult to disentangle the exact causes of displacement. Displacement reported to have been caused by a takeover could in fact have been caused by the economic downturn of the acquired company; in other words, displacement may have occurred whether or not the firm was taken over by another (personal communication with Paul Flaim, Displaced Workers Division, Bureau of Labor Statistics, June 1989). Nonetheless, there is a consensus that extraordinary numbers of managerial and executive employees have been displaced as a result of corporate restructuring processes in the 1980s.

Reflecting a relatively new and noteworthy attempt to force white-collar managerial workers to pay for corporate hard times, firms faced with inescapable competitive pressures have extracted concessions in job regularity, security, and status from these employees. Corporations targeted the management employment contract: reports of wage freezes, salary cuts, newly instituted pay-for-merit systems, suspension of bonuses, and forced early retirement packages for staff and line managerial and professional employees emanated regularly from the corporate headquarters of restructuring firms such as Xerox, U.S. Steel (now USX), du Pont, American Telephone and Telegraph (AT & T), Hewlett-Packard, Ford, General Motors, and Texaco, to name but a few.[9]

Overall, cutbacks in the ranks and employment conditions of middle management are part of a larger, permanent shift in the American employment framework. Industrial relations and organizations specialists argue that American firms, now cognizant of an end to uninterrupted economic growth and of the need for greater control over costs, can no longer afford to sustain bureaucratic (Pfeffer and Baron 1988) or industrial (Kochan, Katz, and McKersie 1986; Osterman 1988) models of control over employees. Those models, in both unionized and nonunionized, blue- and white-collar settings, include implicit and explicit guarantees of job security, clear-cut ca-

9. These reports do not always distinguish sufficiently between corporate staff management cuts and operations-level management cuts, although it is clear that cutbacks are occurring at both levels. The case study presented here addresses changes in operations-level management rather than corporate staff level (see n. 12 for fuller explication). A partial list of articles in the business press and management periodicals summarizing the weakening of the managerial labor market includes *Businessweek* (20 December 1982; 25 April 1983a; 25 April 1983b; 4 August 1986; 12 September 1988); *Fortune* (20 September 1982; 6 February 1984; 28 October 1985a; 2 February 1987; 2 March 1987); *New York Times* (23 June 1982; 17 October 1982b; 22 March 1987; 24 January 1988); *Wall Street Journal* (29 November 1984; 26 May 1987a); Levine (1986); and Willis (1987). Many of these changes have hit professional workers as well; but because middle managers have a unique role in introducing change in the corporation this study analyzes their position exclusively.

reer paths, stable internal labor markets, and the treatment of labor as a fixed cost. They emerged as a result of varied historical conditions including labor/management conflicts and the extraordinary prosperity of large American firms.

Given the greater uncertainty and struggle for profitability in the 1980s and beyond, these specialists argue, companies now seek to cut back on the practices and expectations associated with the old models. Whether by adopting a militant antilabor approach to extracting concessions, pursuing a cooperative approach to gaining labor's participation in new productivity schemes, or externalizing more of the firm's work force, American corporate management has been unraveling the stable employment relations framework that has been in place for many decades. The trend has only recently exploded at a level "perhaps unequaled since labor relations was transformed by the union movement and legislation associated with the Great Depression" (Osterman 1988, p. 61), an assessment shared by Kochan, Katz, and McKersie (1986).

The fate of workers and managers is similarly, although not always equally, bound up in this trend. For whereas workers and managers both must make concessions in the terms of employment, managers face a wholly new demand: they must retool their social relations with those they manage and take on a unique role in pushing through new corporate conditions.

As corporations adopt drastic cutting measures in attempts to restore profitability to the firm and strive to sustain participation and legitimacy while stable employment patterns become strained and uncertain, top managements look to their middle managers to "manage organizational decline" by engineering layoffs, job cuts, and decreased opportunities for mobility in a sensitive and timely way (Gilmore and Hirschhorn 1983; Bunker and Williams 1986). Maintaining continuity and gaining employee consent to corporate restructuring processes present significant organizational and personnel challenges to those running the American corporation. This is especially difficult when firms regularly lay off

employees and block once open career paths (Osterman 1988).
As firms restructure, lower levels of managers become the
crucial link between new earnings objectives and the ongoing
reproduction of daily productive activities. In this domain of
responsibility, top management has tried to position middle
management as agents of restructuring, to get them to mediate corporate restructuring processes as they affect daily
work relations.

New Corporate Ideologies:
Scapegoating Middle Management

At the very time that corporate restructuring processes eliminate important conditions for exercising genuine entrepreneurialism, corporate top managements and management
consultants fervently advocate the notion of entrepreneurial
management to their middle managerial personnel. The popular antibureaucratic, pro-entrepreneurial ideology is especially ironic because this "progressive" framework neatly
dovetails with the dismissal of middle management. Culti-
vated by the "experts"—management consultants, authors,
pundits, and academics—the roots of the new ideology of entrepreneurial management are independent of the actual
practices and beliefs of the managers who are its targets. Despite or perhaps because of this disjuncture, the ideology has
acquired the status of corporate gospel.

Dominant corporate ideologies that specify how managers
should act provide only limited insights into what managers
actually do and think (Nichols 1980). At the same time, however, such corporate ideologies and their expression in managerial "success" books and speeches herald new expectations of managers as well as changes occurring inside the
corporation. In this case, what appears to be a positive and
sincere appeal to middle managerial professionalism is little
more than a tool business leaders increasingly use to obscure
and justify deep-rooted structural changes, many of which

undermine an implicit contract middle managers have had with large corporations.

In this counterintuitive framework, the new entrepreneurial manager should act deftly and flexibly inside even the largest of the country's corporations.[10] Typical of the "progressive" management literature, *In Search of Excellence*, for example, urges the new entrepreneurial manager to eschew bureaucratic and centralized organizational structures and promote instead a "leaner," decentralized work environment in which managers can act rapidly and flexibly (Peters and Waterman 1984).

Entrepreneurial managers have, among other projects, the mission to identify and weed out unproductive, overmanagerialized areas within the corporation, even in their own work unit. Indeed, the sign of the true corporate entrepreneur is his or her willingness to subordinate individual interests to the good of the firm. Thus Kanter (1986) suggests that "the rising managerial entrepreneurs even work themselves out of jobs" when they see particular areas of the firm that have outlasted their value and are providing diminishing returns to the organization (p. 20). The new ideology also clouds the import of managers' role in getting rid of purportedly superfluous employees. Specifically, the "good" entrepreneurial manager should assume responsibility for managing out the jobs of others.

The allegedly progressive, antibureaucratic ideology of entrepreneurial management follows nearly a decade in which experts have consistently blamed American management for the contemporary decline in American productivity and competitiveness. Hayes and Abernathy (1980) precipitated this thinking by publishing, in the *Harvard Business Review*, a criticism that has engaged the attention of business and academic leaders alike. They see the contemporary management

10. This contrasts with an earlier ideology advocating independent entrepreneurialism wherein individuals could find success outside existing organizations (Biggart 1983).

"gospel" of analytic detachment from real products and markets, shortsightedness in financial planning, and hyperabstraction as "playing a major role in undermining the vigor of American industry."

Other business observers echoed this criticism but redirected it toward middle management. Calling his claim an "awkward" one, Judson (1982) argues that "management ineffectiveness is by far the single greatest cause of declining productivity in the U.S." (p. 93). Monsen and Saxberg (1977) point to managers' values and attitudes as a key to America's declining productivity, rather than more common explanations such as low levels of capital investment. And Reich (1983) and Ginzberg and Vojta (1985), liberal policy analysts and human resources experts, similarly call for greater flexibility and innovation in the ranks of American middle management, claiming that the modern corporate enterprise has become overmanagerialized and rigid.[11]

The emergence of a new, presumably optimistic ideology of management does not signal the end of an era of blaming management for America's productivity ills. On the contrary, these are two versions of the same theme. The new corporate ideology, promulgated by experts and business leaders, turns management on itself, providing the philosophical underpinnings and organizational mechanisms by which middle managers can attack management bloat and bureaucratic management styles.

11. Indeed, corporate raiders such as Carl Icahn, who gained tremendous notoriety as a leader of corporate restructuring, exploit the theme of "overly bureaucratic, middle management bloat" to justify their corporate raiding activities. Icahn claims that "layers of bureaucrats reporting to bureaucrats must end," and that his purpose in raiding corporations is simply to force the clean-up of murky organizational structures (*Businessweek*, 27 October 1986). See also then deputy secretary of the treasury Richard Darmon's call for scaling down the insidious "American corpocracy" (*New York Times*, 8 November 1986).

Situating Middle Management Historically

Merger and acquisition activities have forced hundreds of thousands of managerial and administrative workers out of American corporations; corporate leaders have excised innumerable layers of bureaucratic, managerial "fat" and are effectively undoing the prevailing bureaucratic model of employment in our largest firms; and a new corporate ideology aids the war on management bloat and bureaucracy by appealing to middle managers not only to manage but also to become enthusiastic leaders of restructuring processes. Worsened employment conditions indicate that middle managers themselves have become objects and agents: new targets in a well-known agenda in which the struggle to maintain corporate profitability leads to no-holds-barred strategies for maximizing earnings.

Surface impressions, however, fail to answer questions about the actual structure and organization of middle management. They tell us little about what happens inside the firm, as thousands of managers apparently disappear, and as corporations develop new organizational forms to carry out production objectives. They tell us little about the effect of "managerial restructuring" on the configuration of authority relations within firms, or about the intramanagerial politics that result from corporate and managerial restructuring. And finally, they relay little understanding of the intersection between structural and ideological change inside the large corporation.

The partial perspective available so far begs for a fuller and more fundamental analysis of changes in American management. These tendencies compel us to ask: do the surface changes indicate something structural and deep-rooted about the way firms and industries are reconstituting middle management? Historians of corporate structure and behavior have written thousands of pages on the origins of the large American corporation and its particular organization of middle management. Alfred Chandler's work provides perhaps the most impressive historical research on this corporate formation. Since the conclusions of *Strategy and Structure* (1962) form an important point of departure for understanding the possibility of a contemporary reconstitution of middle management, they must briefly be considered.

In Chandler's view, the centralized firm of the early twentieth century posed a historical challenge to corporate leaders and their administrative practices. He chronicles business leaders' increasing difficulties in coordinating output and distribution as firms moved from competitive, market-controlled institutions to oligopolistic and monopolistic ones. The centralized corporate form of earlier times became a stumbling block to maximizing new opportunities.

Top managements facing this situation attempted to contain global uncertainty while increasing the discretion of the lower levels of the firm. They internalized control over production and distribution through vertical integration and diversification. The consequences of these new administrative methods were paramount. The organization of production and distribution would critically determine whether American industry could move forward into this new stage of corporate growth.

Appropriate management structures could enable corporations to move into new product markets and profits. With the right organizational device, managers could achieve more effective communication between and coordination of diverse units within one firm, design planning procedures to maximize the use of all corporate resources (facilities, personnel, machinery, raw materials), and regularize operations and production processes. Using bureaucratic administrative systems, all aspects of production and distribution would be internalized within the corporation rather than subjected to relatively unpredictable market forces.

The decentralized multidivisional corporate structure, the elements of which were so ingeniously explored by Pierre du Pont and others, freed owners and top managers from daily tactical decisions so that they could concentrate on strategic decision making about diversification and international expansion. Divisional- and operations-level managers were given the authority, facilities, and guidelines to make daily tactical decisions.[12] In *The Visible Hand,* Chandler describes how growth was predicated on hiring "dozens and then hundreds" of lower- and middle-level managers whose work and positions inside operating units "didn't vary a lot from those men who owned and managed a single independent factory or office" (Chandler 1977, p. 411). For Chandler, the bureaucratic corporate structure centralized strategic authority at the top of the firm but contained an organizational basis for decentralized, semi-autonomous action at lower levels of the firm.[13]

12. A word about Chandler's definition of middle-level management is in order. In *Strategy and Structure* administrative level managers engage in long-term planning and appraisal; they coordinate and plan the overall work of the enterprise as well as the distribution of resources across units and divisions in the firm (Chandler 1962, pp. 8–9). Operations managers within units oversee day-to-day production; they conduct operational duties within the framework of policies set by headquarters. Chandler identifies two types of decision making that are generally the responsibility of these levels of management: strategic and tactical decision making, respectively.

In *The Visible Hand* Chandler explores in more detail the historically specific ranks of what he calls middle management that grew in the context of multidivisional, diversified firms (the subject of *Strategy and Structure*). Middle management, Chandler argues, had a unique position in the growth of these firms: it was middle managers who really made close coordination between administrative and operations management possible by "monitor(ing) the performance of the operating units under their command and coordinat(ing) the flow of materials through them" (1977, p. 377). These middle managers were organizationally located between divisions and top executives.

Finally, Chandler at times uses these management categories interchangeably. In certain case studies in *Strategy and Structure,* for example, he refers to operations managers within units as middle managers—not working on the line of production but themselves involved in planning and administration within their own operations area. In the popular and scholarly management literature one finds the term "middle management" used inconsistently to refer to both managers within units and managers between divisions and headquarters.

13. As many have argued, centralization does not preclude decentralization and indeed they are often necessary correlates in or-

Such administrative systems gave corporate enterprises the means to grow into global multi-industrial empires because they coordinated and expanded output. Thus as corporate leaders built a multidivisional decentralized organizational structure, they laid the groundwork for the rise of new ranks of managers. Jacoby (1984) notes a steady increase in the ratio of administrative to production employees between 1880 and 1920 as a result of the creation of a new structure of management, including engineers, personnel and middle managers (pp. 24–25), a trend that continued as the numbers of managerial and supervisory employees increased disproportionately throughout the twentieth century (Melman 1951; Bendix 1956, pp. 211–226).[14]

As Melman (1983, chap. 4) points out, the spread of the multiunit decentralized corporation played a "strategic" part in the growth of administrative and managerial employees. Managers in divisions were given considerable authority in a context of economic growth and the internationalization of markets. As strategic managements multiplied their managerial control systems to cope with corporate growth (between central headquarters and divisions), the intensity and scope of decision making broadened and multiplied within divisions. This change leads Melman to note that the ratio of

---

ganizational structures. Child (1977), for example, points out that formalized procedures specify how tasks will be delegated, although not necessarily how they will be performed. Dawson and McLoughlin (1986) argue that the decentralization of decisions to supervisory roles is not inconsistent with an increase in higher-level managerial management control. Mintzberg (1979) finds that horizontal decentralization (within a unit) may coexist with vertical centralization (between units) and vice versa (chap. 11). See Kruisinga (1954) on the relationship between organizational centralization and decentralization.

14. Edwards (1979) identifies another factor leading to the enormous increase of administrative employees: firms had to employ more and more managers and supervisors to control workers. His class-centered analysis is compatible with the organizational-structure explanations of theorists such as Chandler and Melman, although the latter essentially ignore the social relations of the firm.

administrative to production workers, which doubled between 1899 and 1947, doubled again in the postwar period: between 1947 and 1977 the ratio grew to 43 administrative employees for every 100 production employees (Melman 1983, p. 71). As the size of central administrative offices grew, so too did the administrative ratio within units.

Others confirm these conclusions. Researchers have conflicting hypotheses about the relationship between corporate size and administrative ratios but tend to agree about the relationship between corporate form—multiunit or multidivisional decentralized organization—and the growth of administrative, managerial ranks. Delehanty (1968, chaps. 3, 4) summarizes the research, arguing that certain corporate forms call for greater numbers of nonproduction employees and, conversely, that higher administrative ratios allow oligopolistic firms to handle possible expansion (Delehanty 1968, p. 100). In other words, the multilayered bureaucratic structure of management has enabled employers to increase profitability in a context of expansion and capital consolidation.

For the better part of the twentieth century, middle-level managers in decentralized bureaucratic structures have had a unique role in the firm. Not solely constrained by shop floor production politics, they possessed greater managerial latitude than the foreman of the nineteenth-century drive system of management. But neither were they constrained by top management. Rather, they had organizational room to judge how best to manage production and consent to production objectives.

Organization theorists and corporate observers must now determine whether this form of management, so characteristic of twentieth-century industry, will survive. The United States has entered a new era of capital accumulation, one in which previously stable markets are now uncertain, in which corporations cannot count on continued economic growth and prosperity. Both conditions were vital to the spread of the multidivisional, decentralized corporation. As corporations adopt new profitability strategies, reorganizing their "bases of accumulation" (Henderson and Castells 1987), the semi-autonomous management apparatus may become part of the corporate past. Top managements are striving to gain more control over costs and operations and reduce the autonomy and discretion of different production divisions; in so doing they are centralizing historically decentralized corporate forms. Dismantling or, at the very least, restructuring the management hierarchy is a logical corollary, one that I explore in depth in this book.

A secondary organizational concern of this book is whether or not America's middle managers are the principle source of corporate size, rigidity, and lack of competitiveness, as many currently claim. This concern follows the tradition of Bowles, Gordon, and Weisskopf (1984, chap. 6), who ask a similar question about American workers. Using impressive quantitative measures, these authors argue that "the social costs of corporate power" more adequately explain declining productivity than the familiar claim that "labor's wage gains have outstripped productivity growth" (p. 35). Understanding the sources of America's competitive dilemma will take us a long way toward understanding the solutions to our current economic and organizational problems.[15]

Research in a Restructuring Corporation

These visible institutional and ideological developments indicate important changes in the work and authority relations of management within large U.S. corporations. As life in corporate America undergoes powerful transformations after decades of economic growth and dominance, we must identify and explain in greater depth the reorganization of management, as well as managers' responses to the organizational changes surrounding them.

15. For other examples of this tradition see Perlo (1982), Darby (1984), Juravich (1985), and Block (1986), who, for different reasons, criticize the "scapegoating workers for declining productivity" thesis.

Should we assume that middle managers compliantly tend the aftershocks of restructuring in their daily management practices? Do they turn into efficient entrepreneurial managers who, when they have fulfilled their mission for the corporation, manage themselves out of jobs? Has the large corporation found the appropriate organizational responses to adapt to the absence of bureaucratic layers?

To answer these questions I conducted an in-depth case study of a large banking firm that began restructuring its operations and personnel in the early 1980s. American Security Bank's story contains important lessons about the rise and decline of U.S. economic enterprises and the consequences of this transformation for the structure and organization of middle management.[16] American Security Bank is a multidivisional financial services institution that represents perhaps the quintessential location of the postindustrial managerial or professional employee working in a large, paternalistic, white-collar firm. Renowned for its profitability and rapid growth, this California bank seemed an excellent place to study the impact of corporate restructuring on management. American Security's organizational past mirrored, to a significant degree, the organizational histories of major industrial concerns throughout the twentieth century (see Chandler 1962). Moreover, in the early 1980s American entered a phase of financial and organizational contraction and centralization shared by many other historically oligopolistic firms.

In 1985, midway through my research, American Security Bank was hit by profit losses of a staggering magnitude, a crisis that served to intensify the processes unfolding before me. But although American Security's crisis was severe, it did not negate the conditions that the bank shared with other restructuring corporations. The *extreme* corporate profitability crisis only hastened processes already set in motion several years earlier by a *general* profitability crisis. The causes of American Security Bank's struggle for survival in the 1980s

16. The name American Security Bank is a pseudonym.

were at once unique, rooted in the bank's particular business history, and representative, rooted in the same economic-industrial context and set of growth strategies as other large U.S. firms.

In 1985 and 1986, I conducted sixty in-depth, open-ended interviews with bank employees and used a survey to collect demographic and occupational data. I interviewed thirty-five middle managers and supervisors in three production sites in the bank (in the branch system, the computer development division, and the credit card center); ten management development personnel, including three employees who ran the management seminars ("trainers"); and fifteen middle managers in assorted other functional areas, including six working in loan centers. In 1987, I conducted follow-up interviews with five key managers to cross-check and update my understanding of the structural changes and managerial behaviors in American Security Bank.[17] Interviews took place at each individual's work site. Many interviewees took me on extensive tours of their offices, allowing me to observe the details of their production process and to speak with nonmanagerial employees about their job tasks.

I was an involved observer at two week-long management retraining seminars in 1985 and a noninvolved observer at two human resources staff meetings, each lasting between two and three hours.[18] Finally, I spent dozens of hours in the bank library, poring over documentary sources such as in-house management newsletters, management development train-

17. The sample of interviewed managers included 27 women (45 percent) and 33 men (55 percent): three black men, one Hispanic and one Asian man and two Asian women. All others were Caucasian. The average age of the managers I interviewed was 37.9 years and the average salary was a little under $42,000 (in a range that went up to $65,000; three managers reported making "$65,000 or more"). All interviewees were guaranteed confidentiality and are referred to by pseudonyms.

18. See the Appendix for a discussion of involved observation at the management training seminars. The Appendix also includes demographic information about seminar participants.

ing material, employee newspapers, annual reports, and numerous business and trade publications.

The middle managers who were the focus of this study worked in three major divisions of the bank. In all cases middle managers managed other managers or supervisors; they were located below divisional-level management, yet above other managers and supervisors in individual work sites. Responsible for coordinating the daily operations and personnel policies of the firm, these middle managers carried out directives formulated by the bank's top or "strategic" managers—those who determine corporate policies and direction. Thus, corresponding to Chandler's definition of *operations* middle managers (1962; see n. 12), I define middle managers as those *within* divisions, directly involved in planning and coordinating the production of services that are specific to their own units (see also Starbuck 1965, p. 512). Middle managers, in this conceptualization, do not have a formal, institutionalized role in determining investment or growth strategies; nevertheless, their actions can have a very decisive effect on the range of strategies available to top management.

The organization of this book is as follows: Chapter 2 provides the historical backdrop explaining why and how, in the 1980s, American Security Bank's top managers targeted middle managers as the agents and objects of corporate restructuring. This chapter documents how top, or strategic, management, pursuing an extensive agenda for growth and profitability for the better part of the twentieth century, developed a decentralized organizational apparatus by which the firm's middle level of managers could maximize expansion opportunities.

The decentralized bureaucracy, however, ultimately led to a crisis in accountability and control. In the dramatically changed market, technological, and regulatory environment of the late 1970s, top management of American Security Bank had to contract this organizational machinery by recentralizing and consolidating major parts of the bank's functions.

Much of that reorganization affected the bank's thousands

of middle managers directly. Many of their units were reorganized, centralized, and automated. Not only were their own jobs ultimately in question but, in the initial stages of the reorganization effort, managers were singled out as the arbiters of organizational change within the multiple work sites throughout this massive corporation. Chapter 2 explores the dimensions of the new restructuring agenda for middle managers: the impact of corporate restructuring on different divisions in the corporation, the introduction of a strategy of coercive autonomy, and middle managers' new mission to increase productivity with fewer employees and to reduce the bank's personnel by managing out a new socially defined category of "poor performers."

Strategic management attempted to galvanize managers ideologically to the new corporate agenda by requiring all middle managers to attend a series of "retraining" seminars. Chapter 3 analyzes those seminars. The chapter looks at the social processes and pedagogical discourse used to teach managers a new corporate culture, which would allegedly realign their behavior with the changing competitive environment. Specifically, the new cultural platform criticized American Security's middle managers for their unproductive bureaucratic management styles and called for the implementation of new innovative and entrepreneurial management. As rule-following bureaucrats, middle managers were informed, they had blocked the profitability of the firm. But as leaders and facilitators following their managerial instincts and using new management techniques, they could take risks and assume responsibility for improving the competitive position of the bank.

In the seminars, middle managers rejected the new agenda of coercive autonomy and its implications for the micropolitics of management in everyday work sites. They responded negatively to the ways the new techniques would undermine them rather than enable them to maintain or gain the consent of the employees they managed. Although they did not disagree with the need for effective practices to set the corporation back on the track of profitability, their vision of how that could be achieved diverged from the vision of strategic management.

After analyzing middle managers' responses to the training seminars, I move on, in Chapters 4, 5, and 6, to analyze managers' actions in their everyday work practices. Using interview and observational data, I compare the impact of corporate restructuring on middle managerial job tasks and social relations in three major functions in the bank (branch banking, credit, and computer systems development). By considering variables such as the functional importance of the division in the restructuring firm, the status of each division's production process, and the degree of managerial autonomy, I identify the organizational changes that opened up or constrained different managerial responses to the corporate transformation. Chart 1 presents a schematic framework for explaining middle managers' actions in the context of restructuring. The analysis in Chapters 4 through 6 will conclude by filling in this schema with concrete descriptions of managers' positional opportunities and constraints. In other words, these chapters trace ways in which restructuring shaped and created different domains of managerial action.

By contrasting three different work sites, Chapters 4 through 6 debunk the notions that managers acted irrationally in their opposition to the new corporate agenda or that they simply acted as the agents of capital and executed the tenets of the new agenda as a weapon against the bank's employees. If they carried out the restructuring agenda as formulated by top management, middle managers confronted a significant dilemma: the purportedly meritocratic but in fact coercive management methods would strip them of their ability to maintain consent to the ongoing reproduction of their production areas. I argue that these managers did extensively use their managerial judgment or "instincts" to manage, but that they did so to ward off the draconian aspects of the new corporate agenda. In different ways, middle managers circumvented strategic management's demands, their respective

Chart 1.   Corporate Restructuring and Management Action

Dimensions of the restructuring process that create organizational opportunities and domains of action for managers (listed in order of significance):

---

(1) Strategic importance of the division as the bank restructures (contraction or expansion?)

(2) Status of middle management (elimination?)

(3) Status of production processes in different divisions (standardized, automated, or rationalized?)

(4) Sources of managerial autonomy (degree and direction of the expropriation of managerial discretion?)

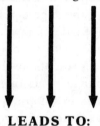

LEADS TO:

Different options available to middle managers to reinterpret and resist strategic management policies; domains of managerial action:

---

(1) Raising employee productivity or getting employees to leave the firm ("managing up or managing out")

(2) Intensification of on-site vs. vertical negotiations

(3) Offensive vs. defensive strategies

---

organizational latitude shaping their ability to reinterpret or reject them.

Middle managers managed according to a different sense of the corporate interest. Whereas strategic management advocated arbitrary management methods and a new corporate culture to achieve a quick turnaround of the bank, middle management perceived high costs in this quick-fix perspective. Middle managers' sense of what best served the corporate interest emphasized practices that could achieve a more gradual turnaround; their goal was to preserve the existing framework of consent, using that framework to achieve new goals and maintain long-term corporate viability.

Finally, in addition to delineating the structural differences between managers and the subsequent variation in managerial responses, Chapters 4 through 6 also point to the emergence of a new arrangement of production that depended on centralized organizational and technological control. Despite differences in the pace and degree of restructuring managerial autonomy, all of these production centers were moving toward centrally controlled forms of production that, in top management's ideal vision, would operate without intervening levels of managers. This shift represented strategic management's intention to control semi-autonomous tactical management decisions more closely. Thus I locate middle managers' responses within the transition from a decentralized to a centralized corporate form.

The final chapter moves away from the case study of American Security Bank to consider the larger agenda to restructure work processes, the organization of management, and corporations in the United States. Using the case study material and other data, I look at the convergence of three levels of change in American corporations: changes in production processes (both physical organization and employment patterns), changes in management, and changes in the structure of the corporation. Changes in the position of management are inseparable from changes in the position of workers in the United States; in turn, the fate of both these groups is bound up in that of the American corporation. Understanding this convergence will allow students of business, labor, and corporate organization to generalize about the future of work, management, and industrial relations in the United States.

2

The Business of Banking

It ought to be axiomatic in the world of business that
one century's victorious strategy is apt to become
the next century's strategy for failure.
John Hoerr, *And the Wolf Finally Came*

Strategic management's attack on stodgy, "bureaucracy-hun-
gry" middle managers is ironic. American Security Bank's
historical record suggests that it was in fact hyper-entrepre-
neurialism, exercised by top management, that gave rise to
many of the bank's current problems. If middle managers really
were rigid, bureaucratically oriented actors, American's successes would almost certainly have been more modest.

This chapter analyzes the relationship between American
Security Bank's growth and the decentralized bureaucratic
management structure that was a vehicle for that growth.[1]
The relationship between growth strategies and corporate
structure frames the central theoretical core of this book: the
behavior of the firm structures and restructures management
and explains the context in which managers can and do manage. The firm's behavior also provides the backdrop to the

1. Bank reports, an extensive literature search of commentary on
the bank in business and trade publications (including the *Wall Street
Journal, New York Times, Businessweek,* and *Fortune*), *Moody's Bank
and Finance Manual* (selected years between 1930 and 1986),
Congressional Banking and Housing hearings, and data from interviews with bank officials were used to analyze American Security's
growth strategies over the last five decades.

politics of restructuring that emerged in the 1980s and explains why middle management became the target of those corporate changes.

Banking industry commentators have suggested that federal deregulation policies of the late 1970s and early 1980s contributed strongly to the decline of American Security's profits. The bank's strategic management also invoked this explanation to justify demanding changes in middle management productivity. Increased competition resulting from looser federal regulation of interest rates and the entrance of new banking and financial service firms, they argued, would undermine the high profitability experienced by American over the past decades. A general, industrywide experience cannot by itself explain American Security's decline, however. A more plausible explanation rests in the particular organizational form and growth strategies that ultimately limited the bank's ability to respond to an environmental change such as deregulation.

A historical study of American Security Bank's corporate form illuminates the ways in which Chandler's (1962) model of diversification and decentralization is an appropriate one for understanding the organizational developments of non-manufacturing, nonindustrial firms.[2] As it did for many industrial enterprises, the decentralized corporate form enabled the bank, over many decades, to pursue strategies of geographical expansion, product diversification, and multi-divisionalization. Challenged by shrinking markets in the 1970s and 1980s, however, American's decentralized bureaucracy faced important limits. Thus this study also points to the his-

2. McClellan (1981) similarly applies Chandler's model to banking firms. Many may be reluctant to draw parallels between industrial and banking concerns, viewing the banking industry as a unique case because it has been regulated for many decades. Although it is an important variable, regulation in and of itself does not explain the organizational development of banks or of banks' particular profitability strategies. The evidence from this case study suggests that the organizational histories of banks are closely linked to those of industrial firms.

torical limitations of Chandler's model. If the current era of capital and industrial restructuring transforms the large de-centralized firm, then organization theorists must prepare to consider a new corporate form.

Domestic Expansion

The size of a bank's deposit base determines the degree to which banks can realize profits through lending and invest-ment.[3] Between World War I and the early 1960s, American Security Bank erected the infrastructural means to develop a huge base of consumer deposits: its branch banking system, spread throughout the state of California.

American Security Bank's rapid expansion was in part due to a prosperous, burgeoning economy. California was one of the fastest growing states in the country: between 1940 and 1950, 19 percent of the U.S. population increase occurred in California, with an increase of nearly four million people. American Security's growth, however, was not an "organic" one, in which the bank simply responded to increasing mar-ket demand. Rather, American Security Bank's lending poli-cies fueled California's growth, especially in the crucial areas of agriculture and housing. This fact is important to under-standing American Security's growth: to profit from its large deposit base, American had to sell its product—to loan out that money quickly, at rates higher than the cost of its main-tenance. Two developments enabled American Security to do this: the decentralized character of the branch system and aggressive lending policies.

3. The majority of U.S. commercial banks' total operating in-come consists of income from loans and loan-related activities (Roussakis 1984, p. 308). The size of a loan portfolio is restricted only by a bank's capital structure (there must be adequate liquidity and loan loss provisions), and by the amount of money the bank can ac-cumulate to lend out; hence, increasing the deposit base is a major source of a bank's ability to realize profits.

By the 1960s American Security Bank had developed an extensive branch system, each offering a full range of services.[4] (The bank founded some of its hundreds of branches and acquired and merged with others.) In a system described by the business press as "regimented autonomy," every manager and loan officer within American Security's branches possessed full authority to grant loans. Although the bank's central finance committee established the lending limit of each branch, actual decision making about borrowers was localized within branches.

That "autonomy" of the branch system made the bank's lending structure adaptable to many different regional factors existing around the state, giving it an ability to move very rapidly to secure business. A lending official in Los Angeles might know little about rural collateral, land appraisal, or how seasonal factors could affect a Fresno or Salinas borrower's ability to repay loans; to have to gain approval from such an administrator would significantly hamper American Security's efforts to dominate the lending business. From the bank administration's point of view, each branch manager should think of his or her branch as a bank he or she personally owned and should exercise discretion accordingly.

Indeed, branch managers in general possessed significant authority and responsibility. They were trained in the area of credit and managed employees in several functional areas within the branch, including credit (lending) and operations (assistant branch managers, merchant and individual ac-

---

4. American Security was able to build this system because California state laws permitted statewide branch banking. As a so-called retail bank, American Security had a large number of smaller transactions, collected through its widely dispersed branch network. Many states prohibited branch banking, as New York did until recently. So-called corporate institutions banked instead with fewer and larger corporate accounts. Compared with the corporate banks, American's rapid ascent into the upper ranks of the banking industry is thus quite remarkable, an indication of the bank's early aggressive search of business. The regulatory environment thus determines the growth strategies available to banks.

count tellers, bookkeepers, and back-room payments processors). Furthermore, their lending work made branch managers modestly important community figures and linked the bank to regional economic prosperity in a relatively personalized fashion.

Thus the branch officials themselves had to be able to determine the creditworthiness of borrowers. With branch profitability calculated on loan-to-deposit ratios, branch managers were authorized and encouraged to increase sales of loans. Rapidity of decision making, made possible by the decentralized branch structure, greatly boosted this effort. The low cost of keeping deposits also promoted profitability. Regulation Q, legislated in the 1930s to stabilize the banking industry, placed a ceiling on deposit interest rates, allowing American Security (like other banks) to realize significant profits as they loaned their deposit money out at higher rates.

Expansion was further fueled by the existence of guidelines with which managers could make operations and personnel decisions—what Chandler (1962) calls tactical decisions (p. 11). The *Standardized Procedures Manual* outlined the centralized parameters within which managers could maneuver and make decisions appropriate to specific regional and market factors. Data on branch activities were forwarded to and monitored by central offices governing Northern and Southern California; these offices were responsible for updating bank policies and sending them to all branches. Personnel management similarly was decentralized and coordinated at the same time: each branch manager was able to hire, fire, and distribute wage increases within the salary matrix designed by central personnel. Centralized guidelines established the limits of decision making in this decentralized bureaucracy.

Any attempt to subject the growing number of branches to more centralized control would, in the eyes of the bank's strategic management, lead to monumental problems. In the late 1950s an executive vice-president was quoted in the business press, arguing, "If we tried direct central supervision over 659 branches spread out over 158,000 square miles, the administrative costs would be terrific, and the service would be terrible."

Bank officials noted the enormity of the personnel problem. In one year typical of this high-growth period, for example, over fifty branches were opened, each with the same hierarchical layers of management, tellers, bookkeepers, loan officers, and clerical help; strategic management predicted they would open thirty to forty branches with similar labor requirements in each of the following years. Expansion, and the subsequent corner on California's deposit and lending base, was sufficiently profitable to justify such duplication.[5]

At the same time that American Security Bank was extending this structure throughout the state, the bank was marketing novel loan products. Their installment loan plan and a successful credit card program broadened the bank's small consumer loan base. American Security aggressively sold loans: advertising campaigns used newspapers, radio, and billboards to announce milestones such as "Today 266 cars will be financed by American Security" and "Every five minutes another American Security–financed car."

The institutional structure for which American Security Bank became famous was firmly in place by the early 1960s. The decentralized branch banking system was predicated on a semi-autonomous management structure that allowed the bank to pursue and maximize market opportunities. Tactical had been separated from strategic management (Chandler 1962, pp. 8–11): top-level management had created a global, profit-maximizing organizational framework within which middle, branch-level managers had significant latitude to carry out day-to-day operations.

Fueled by its access to California deposits and by its insistent sale of money, American Security became not only a phe-

---

5. Banking productivity studies have shown, however, that "the spread of branch banking somewhat retards productivity improvement"; the scale of economy diminishes productivity as more resources are required per unit of output (Brand and Duke 1982, p. 19).

nomenally profitable firm but one with a significant role in developing entire new systems of lending and credit that spurred the California economy. This role was a result of aggressive, expansionary decision making on the part of strategic management. American's growth was "purchased," carved out with organizational and lending schemes that would inextricably bind the bank to the very heart of the state's economy.[6]

International Expansion

Reaching significant limits to growth and profitability in California, American Security Bank turned, as did many banks in the 1960s, to foreign expansion. American Security's international growth rates were notable. At the close of World War II American Security had one overseas branch, but by 1970 it had dozens of foreign branches and well over a hundred foreign banking subsidiaries.

6. Using a figure derived from bank documents, one source reported that the ratio of American's loans to deposits was little over 45 percent in 1939, while the ratio for the rest of the banking industry was 32.5 percent. I have not discussed an additional factor in American Security's growth process, because in this section I simply want to lay out the organizational bases for understanding American's current crisis. During this period, strategic management constantly battled with the Comptroller of the Currency and Federal Reserve Board over its expansionary policies. Each new branch required licensing, and many instances can be found in which the Comptroller challenged American's growth because of concerns about monopolization and about the soundness of the bank's capital structure. Furthermore, strategic management lobbied ceaselessly to reform regulatory laws that prohibited interstate banking. In general, the federal agencies regulate the fiscal health of banks in the Federal Reserve system. The Comptroller of the Currency, an arm of the Treasury Department, routinely audits bank assets, capital structure, and loan portfolios and monitors the mechanisms used by senior management to ensure financial soundness. These mechanisms include policies and controls governing loan approval, reviews, and classification, determination of loan loss provision, management information systems for relaying weaknesses and strengths in loan approval systems, and loan officer compensation systems.

Two aspects of the international-expansion phase are striking. First, American Security Bank began pursuing international business comparatively later than other major banks. Banking observers expressed some skepticism about whether there was really room for another major U.S. competitor, particularly one that lacked experience with large accounts. Second, the bank's late entry led to questionable strategies for international profitability. One major business publication pointed out that American Security Bank initially planned to enter countries with limited capital and banking facilities and small economic risks. As it entered an increasingly crowded market, that cautious intent changed to the goal of being "flexible" to the international conditions that it encountered. American hoped to carve out a specialized market, to meet unique needs of corporate customers.

It is possible that to some degree American Security Bank positioned itself in niches where other banks would not go. American, *Businessweek* suggested, gained a reputation for being overly liberal with long-term credit, indicating much greater lenience with borrowers' creditworthiness. Despite the uncertainty, however, the international market was nevertheless a profitable one. Banks faced comparatively few restrictions on their overseas activities; profit margins on local currency loans in many countries were high compared with U.S. margins; and banks were taxed at lower rates.

The rapidity of American Security's international growth suggests an extremely aggressive expansion plan, paralleling earlier infrastructural domestic growth rates. Although American was among the last of the top banks to go international, by 1970 it ranked high among U.S. banks on the international scene. By that time, over 20 percent of the bank's profits were from overseas operations.

Domestically, strategic management no longer depended solely on rapidly expanding the California infrastructure. Rather it intensified existing profit-seeking activities and implemented organizational measures that extended the bank's markets. In the mid-sixties, for example, American Security

Bank began negotiating with banks around the country to extend its one-million-member credit card program. By 1970, American Security's highly successful marketing campaign had resulted in increasing the number of credit card holders by several million. Credit card operations earned over 5 percent of the bank's total operating earnings.

The California branch system did grow during this period. By 1970 American Security Bank was one of the leading contenders for California's $50 billion of available deposits.[7] However, the ratio between branch growth and deposit growth had changed. Despite its infrastructural growth, American Security's share of the total available deposits was not increasing. The cost of maintaining its market share rose; branch growth allowed American merely to maintain rather than to expand its position.

In the late 1960s, American Security petitioned for and received approval to establish itself as a one-bank holding company. As a parent company for the bank, the one-bank holding company could sidestep some of the restrictions imposed on banks per se, to diversify into profit-making activities traditionally viewed as outside the scope of commercial banking, such as leasing, insurance, real estate, warehousing, and mutual funds (Roussakis 1984). The organizational arrangement permitted American Security to enlarge the scope and number of profit-making centers.[8]

7. The expansion strategies of most large California banks were visible during this period. California continued to be viewed as a lucrative banking market, with a population increase of 27 percent between 1960 and 1970, and with personal incomes that grew faster than in the United States as a whole. The top seven banks held between them 90 percent of the available deposits.

8. McClellan's (1981) in-depth case studies of "General Bank Corporation" and "Sherman Bank Corporation" demonstrate similar reasoning behind the development of the one-bank holding company. McClellan's is an excellent account of the processes of diversification, shown by Chandler (1962) in industrial concerns, in the banking industry. Seeing profitability as a *secondary* rationale for diversification, McClellan argues that the *primary* cause of banking diversification was "financial vertical integration," through which

Thrusting control of branch operations even further down the bank hierarchy, American Security's leaders adopted a policy of regionalization. Rather than maintain control over policy decisions from centralized headquarter offices, strategic management redistributed responsibility for senior credit authority and staff into regional offices throughout the state. Each regional office controlled eighty to a hundred branches. Bank administrators noted that this was one of the most significant shifts in authority ever implemented in the bank.

By the beginning of the 1970s strategic management had parlayed American Security Bank into a major U.S. bank. Yet the records on American Security's growth strategies suggest a struggle to maintain profitability and a volatility in the successes achieved. American Security had to expend greater resources simply to maintain its market share in California; faced with limits to its own growth in the California market, strategic management had ventured into a crowded international market; and it had acquired the organizational and legal apparatus to seek new nonbanking profit centers. The next era of growth must be viewed as decisive for American Security Bank: strategies of that period represent a response to comparatively limited possibilities for expansion in the context of an increasing struggle for profits.

One Step Forward, Two Steps Back: Growing but Losing Ground

Capitalizing on existing structures and practices, over the next ten years the bank followed a trajectory of profit maximization that had been taking shape for several decades. Between 1970 and 1980 American Security's assets and profits quadrupled, and the number of bank employees doubled to well over 50,000 in yet another aggressive expansion program. In the last five years of the period alone, net income nearly doubled.

---

banks gained access to much needed raw material in the form of new sources of capital (McClellan 1981, pp. 168–169).

These achievements were based on strategies that gave rise in a very dramatic way to the profitability crisis of the 1980s. The institutional and policy apparatus that nurtured those strategies was already firmly in place by 1970. But a new dynamic characterized the 1970s: growth in lending was used to obscure lack of growth in deposit markets. In addition, strategic management maintained high short-term profit margins by neglecting investment that would bolster the long-term health of the bank. It did not invest in technology that the rest of the banking industry was already adopting, nor did it prepare for the forthcoming deregulation of interest rates.

By the mid-seventies, operating authority lay in the hands of unit managers at over one hundred "profit centers" around the world (which included new subsidiaries owned by the bank holding company), while control of capital and important credit decisions remained under the purview of headquarters.[9] Branch managers were given still broader authority over promotions and salaries, while domestic lending officers were given higher loan limits. Lending authority in foreign operations was similarly decentralized: by 1975 only 20 percent of foreign transactions were routed to senior management for approval.

That downward movement of decision making, resulting in the creation of autonomous profit centers, perhaps best explains the enormous increase of personnel that took place during the decade: the number of bank employees nearly doubled. One influential business publication also reported that branch managers were compensated on the basis of size, suggesting that branch managers built up their staffs to imple-

9. Continental Illinois, a bank that also experienced a major crisis in the 1980s, adopted a similar decentralized structure during the same period. In 1972, Continental expanded individual lending officers' authority and removed the loan approval process from a committee framework. Major lending responsibility was delegated to those in the field, resulting in fewer controls and levels of review of loan applications. The purpose was to provide greater flexibility to lending officers, in order to expand the bank's loan portfolio greatly (Miller 1985, p. 14).

ment strategic management imperatives. The bank had established a notable orientation toward increasing revenues and focusing less on daily costs and productivity; that orientation was protected by ongoing growth. In other words, this large and prosperous firm was trading off efficiency for expansion and profitability.[10]

With a massive, decentralized corporation, increased latitude in loan making, and a strategic management that relied on lending as a growth strategy, the bank achieved the zenith of its loan portfolio in the late 1970s. During a brief four-year period, the bank doubled its agricultural lending, accumulating a high concentration of agricultural loans that would make American extremely vulnerable to any collapse of farm property value.

During the same period, the bank extended many billions in foreign loans, often to small borrowers in Latin America and Africa who were considered high credit risks. The bulk of American Security's foreign loans were to private borrowers, compared with other banks' loans to governments and public entities. American Security Bank continued to fill a gap in the international banking scene. International growth was spurred by a special division that served multinational corporations. This multinational unit, set up in the early 1970s, followed the logic of regimented autonomy of the branch system. Multinational account officers reported to a senior vice-president of multinational corporate banking in headquarters. Yet the account officer, located near clients' headquarters around the world, held credit authority, approving or disapproving all credit transactions.

Other organizational policies highlight the shaky foundations of the intensification of lending as the principal growth

10. Many rapidly expanded and prosperous industries have had trade-offs between efficiency and growth. For organizational developments that shaped a similar orientation in other industries see Hodgetts, Lawrence, and Schlesinger (1985) on the trucking industry; on the computer industry, see Greenhalgh, McKersie, and Gilkie (1986); on the telecommunications industry, see Feldman (1986).

strategy. Several large units in California, for example, were making substantial real estate construction loans with little coordination between them. This duplication eventually resulted in great concentration of loans in certain sectors, with a low regard for tracing accountability. An emphasis on amassing assets led to a disregard for quality and for any considerations of how American's huge loan portfolio would survive the coming climate of deregulation. Business observers pointed out that American Security Bank's loan officers tended to be generalists who were spread out across the entire branch system, whereas lending officers of other banks were trained as industrial and sectoral specialists.

The strategy of increasing lending levels is one indication of a short-term perspective on profitability; another is the neglect of technological investment. American Security was slow among the California banks to institute automated teller networks. Furthermore, some information-intensive sectors within the bank were still not computerized. Strategic management's reluctance to reinvest earnings and take a cut in immediate high profit rates meant that the administration of the 1980s would have to take up a big technology slack.

The exceptional profitability of American Security Bank at the end of the seventies masked two problems that extracted severe costs over the following years. American Security's loan portfolio, built on an extremely decentralized lending structure, depended on volume rather than quality. Increasing volume was encouraged by incentive. Strategic management relied on earnings growth in consumer and overseas lending to write off other loan losses; the bank was able to absorb losses throughout the decade without significantly diluting profitability.

Second, profitability was in part fueled by lack of reinvestment. Little if any capital was devoted to improving the existing institution, creating catch-up costs that put a strong damper on earnings in the 1980s. Furthermore, the extensive branch system, on which this bank depended for its huge pool of deposit money, seems to have been neglected. By 1980 American Security's share of California deposits had dropped to under 40 percent; thus the bank's very infrastructure and financial core was weakening. American would also have to contend with its deposit market in the early 1980s, when banks and other financial institutions began aggressively to compete for the core of money American Security had always taken for granted.

Retrenchment and Recentralization: The 1980s

The upward earnings trajectory ended abruptly at the turn of the decade. The chief executive officer who had presided over American Security's phenomenal growth during the 1970s left the bank in 1980, the best earnings year American had ever experienced. When Robert Wedgewood[11] stepped into the position in 1981, one of the first noteworthy events he presided over was the announcement of a steep decline of earnings. That was surely an extremely painful admission for Wedgewood, who had worked his way up through the ranks of American Security Bank over the course of many years. Considered by many to have been perfectly groomed for CEO, his career nurtured and watched carefully over many years, he now faced a financial scenario that departed dramatically from American Security's heyday of economic growth and prosperity.

With the exception of one slightly improved year, bank earnings continued to decline; over the next five and a half years, American Security wrote off billions of dollars in loans in precisely those areas where loans had been concentrated in the 1970s. The bank posted not only the reverse in earnings but also profit losses that raised the specter of Depression-era financial ruin. In a climate in which several major banks had either collapsed or been rescued by federal authorities, developments at American Security precipitated much spec-

11. A pseudonym.

ulation on the part of federal regulators, shareholders, Wall
Street observers, and the public about the possible demise of
the bank.

The large loan losses limited American Security's ability to
maneuver in a deregulating financial services environment.
Regulation Q was phased out, gradually eliminating interest
rate ceilings on deposit accounts. The Garn–St. Germain Act
of 1982 allowed other institutions—savings and loans, credit
unions, manufacturing corporations with finance companies,
and retail firms such as Sears—to engage in activities historically restricted to commercial banks (such as deposit taking,
offering checking accounts and traveler's checks, financing,
and lending) (Roussakis 1984). These developments forced
American Security to compete for more of the California retail market: the bank had to begin paying more for its money
and to develop new products in the form of special accounts
and services.

How would strategic management redress the problematic
profitability strategies of the preceding decades? Unable to
rely any longer on building its infrastructure or lending portfolio to expand profits, top management also had to face the
fact that the extreme decentralization policies of the past had
weakened the bank's financial core.

One painful necessity was at the heart of the 1980s strategy
for recapturing bank profitability: reducing the size and the
decentralized character of the bank branch system. A senior
level "retail action team" was organized to consolidate the
branch system, to cut and redeploy staff, and to reduce the
cost structure of retail banking. The team had to decide which
branches would be closed or stripped down, basing its decisions on factors such as a branch's proximity to other branches,
the cost of the premises (American Security owned some
branch buildings and leased others), and the rate of branch
growth.[12]

12. According to a member of the team whose principal responsibility was to generate data about and plans for closing branches,

To reduce the branch system, the action team closed some branches outright or turned them into "convenience centers" (branches with one or two human tellers, several electronic tellers, and very limited services); it removed various branch functions, centralizing loan making, for example, into lending centers and personnel decision making (promotions, hirings, and raises) into area management groups. Although branch closure did not get under way until late 1983, by the end of 1984 strategic management had closed or consolidated several hundred branches.[13]

Closing branches, however, could only be a partial solution. Unlike firms that have the option of closing down production sites when demand declines or when profit crises prevail (Zipp and Lane 1987), American Security Bank's prosperity depended in many ways on maintaining proximity to customers. Branch closures meant sacrificing customers. And in the face of stiffer competition from other banks, maintaining customers was an important part of regaining American Security's market share. Partly for this reason, strategic management focused more intensely on issues of productivity and overstaffing.

The bank began to target its least and most profitable business operations by identifying and stratifying its consumer markets. For the "mass market," strategic management regrouped lending authority, which had been widely dispersed throughout the branch system, into highly rationalized and depersonalized lending centers. Formerly, anyone entering a

---

profitability was not an exclusive factor for determining branch tenure.

13. Strategic management offered a redeployment program, enabling employees whose jobs were eliminated by branch or division closures to seek other jobs at the bank at a comparable rank and salary and within a specified geographic location. Employees who did not accept another job resigned with a separation package. Employees' fears about redeployment were often a major factor in their decision to leave the bank in the coming years. Redeployment thus to some degree allowed strategic management to reduce staff size without having to do the dirty work of actual layoffs.

branch for a loan would negotiate with an on-site lending officer; in the restructured bank a customer had to do business with any one of a handful of regional loan centers, specialized for auto loans, home loans, and so on. In essence, the retail action team "deskilled" the branch by removing lending activities, thus causing a general degradation of financial services for the less than wealthy.

Affluent customers gained access to personalized lending services when "private banking" and "customized" financial services centers, serving the top 15 percent of American Security customers, were set up in area management groups. These small lending groups catered to privileged customers and offered correspondingly elite financial services such as money market accounts, investment counseling, brokerage and securities services, asset management and financial planning, and personalized lending services.

The economic justification for consumer segmentation was clear. As noted in the bank newspaper, whereas the "mass consumer market" (households with less than $25,000 in annual income, of which the retail action team fretted that it had a disproportionate share) made up 47 percent of available business and only 22 percent of potential profit from the retail market, so-called mid-scale and upscale markets constituted 53 percent of available business but 78 percent of potential profit.

Bank leaders similarly consolidated the international division of the bank by centralizing the most important world banking units and installing one chief administrative officer to oversee them. As they had done with domestic markets, strategic management stratified the bank's international customers and foreign countries into market tiers. Tier 3 consisted of countries with whom American Security wanted to terminate relations; tier 2 customers were to be scaled back; international operations would focus primarily on profitable tier 1 countries.

Within the first few years of the Wedgewood administration, strategic management poured several billion dollars into technology research and development, advancing the technological forces that would lead to domestic and international centralization. The rapid proliferation of automatic tellers testifies to top management's interest in increasing the bank's competitiveness through technology. In 1980 American Security Bank had no electronic teller system; by 1985 American had one of the most extensive systems of any bank in the country.

One very important product of that technological catch-up was SystemsGroup, a new division to develop the bank's technology, which was established in 1983. This center, employing several thousand people, housed numerous projects devoted to integrating the bank's operations and improving information management, data processing, and state, national, and international communication. On the international front, for example, SystemsGroup developed data-base linkages between major bank centers in Europe, Asia, Latin America, and the United States. Strategic management claimed it had no choice but to develop these information and communications linkages, called the "electronic pipeline," given the pressures for profitability and competitiveness. SystemsGroup designed electronic delivery and payments mechanisms for American Security Bank customers, as well as in-house office automation using microcomputers and time-sharing services, all designed to link management together.[14]

Managers as Agents and Objects of Change: Personnel Management in a Contracting Corporation

Organizational restructuring was paralleled in top management's attempt to restructure the behavior and culture of

14. The cost of these rapid innovations subtracted significantly from American's already strained profit margins in the 1980s. Moreover, decreases in personnel caused by paring down the branch system were offset by new employees needed in SystemsGroup and other divisions devoted to improving American Security's position in the financial services market.

middle management. Middle managers were to achieve, in individual work sites, what top management was trying to achieve for the corporation as a whole: a leaner, more productive work force.

Strategic management publicly proclaimed that it would uphold the bank's long-standing "no-layoff" policy. This commitment to paternalistic, lifetime employment patterns seemed to signify that top management refused to make employees suffer the consequences of the reorganization of the bank. Yet along with this explicit commitment, strategic management developed a covert plan for cutting personnel, charging middle managers with "managing up or managing out": increasing productivity or firing new categories of unproductive employees.[15] Thus strategic management looked to managers to take responsibility for managing out so-called unproductive workers (including managers themselves) and simultaneously professed that layoffs would be a policy of last resort.

Managing up did not mean promoting an employee into a higher position; rather it meant raising an employee's productivity in his or her current position. Under a new regime of pay for performance or pay for merit, managers were to parcel out bonuses irregularly for improved results. In this way, strategic management hoped to persuade employees at all levels of the bank to work more productively, rather than reward employees solely by promoting them into the upper levels of the corporation. Pay for performance was a fitting incentive in a corporate climate of decreasing opportunities for mobility.

Also appropriate to the new corporate climate were emphases on the benefits of lateral as opposed to vertical mobility. Corporate personnel touted lateral mobility as an often more attractive option than upward mobility; part of middle

15. All terms marked with an asterisk in this chapter and in Chapter 3 are explained in greater detail in the glossary at the end of the book.

managers' new role in managing contraction was to help managerial and nonmanagerial employees alike see the virtue of developing their careers through horizontal mobility. Since the ideology of open job ladders and promotions constitutes an important mechanism of control, limitations on upward mobility presented a new personnel dilemma for middle managers (Rosenbaum 1979; Greenbaum 1979; Scott 1985).[16]

As the agents of corporate contraction, managers were also to isolate and manage out their "nonperformers," unproductive workers who allegedly drained corporate profitability.[17] But the unproductive workers to be managed out were not simply uncooperative or negligent: in a new definition, the "poor performer" was one who fell at the bottom of a ranked curve (the "Bell curve"*) of employees in each unit. Position on the curve determined whether one should be managed out of the firm. Managing up or out, using this scheme to penalize and push employees, would allegedly give managers the daily, micro-level tools to move American Security from a paternalistic growth-based system of personnel policies to one characterized by diminishing opportunities and promises.

Thus rather than resort to explicit layoffs strategic management used two interim strategies to cut the size of American Security Bank's personnel. It was going to rely on attrition—not only normal attrition but attrition somewhat accelerated by the redeployment program—and on lower-level managers taking an assertive stance toward the bank's allegedly unproductive workers. Oaklander (1982) points out that companies often try to reduce staff by attrition as a prelude

16. Indeed, Rosenbaum (1979) argues that promotions may be a "fundamental determinant of a wide variety of other attitudes and behaviors" within organizations (p. 23). Hall and Isabella (1985) examine the increase of downward and lateral mobility in a context of corporate restructuring and the problems that restricted opportunities pose for managers.

17. See *Fortune* (28 October 1985b) for an account of AT & T's efforts to get managers to use new and special performance ratings to identify certain employees as "expendable."

to layoffs. Managing down through attrition can be time-consuming, however, and companies adopt other methods to accelerate the attrition process (Oaklander 1982, pp. 187–214). Managing out, as a type of disguised layoff, was such an accelerating method.[18]

In addition to serving as agents of corporate change, managers were also the targets of that change. The bank's new corporate culture agenda expressed the contradictory dimensions of middle managers' position. Evoking an ideology of the bank as a rigid, overstaffed, bureaucratic institution, strategic management argued that the bank's current crisis could in part be explained by middle management's behavior. Top management conveniently ignored the fact that organization building at the middle managerial level was an understandable response to strategic management's own growth policies and claimed that the bank had become a stagnant corporate morass because of middle managers' behavior. Over the past decades of growth and allegedly automatic profits, top management argued, middle managers had complacently added more and more employees to their units, neglecting any standards of efficiency or competitiveness. The only way the bank could redress this problem was to transform its managerial culture.

Members of American Security's top management went public about the damaging effects of the disease of "manage-

18. Other big corporations have faced dilemmas inherent in pursuing layoffs. See, for example, IBM's struggle to maintain a no-layoff policy (*Businessweek*, 7 July 1986), and a study of the generally problematic implications of engaging in layoffs (*New York Times*, 15 December 1982). *Dun's Business Month* (July 1985) has openly touted the "no layoff payoff" in large corporations such as Delta Airlines, Digital Equipment, and Hewlett-Packard. The problem of securing loyalty and maintaining efficiency in the context of extensive layoffs was the subject of a cover story in *Businessweek* (4 August 1986) and has been extensively explored from a human resources perspective (e.g., Perry 1986). The framing of corporate loyalty as a current social problem underscores one of the persistent questions of this research: the problem of securing and reproducing consent to corporate objectives.

rial complacency." They, and other commentators, compared the bank's middle management to stifled and overbloated civil service bureaucracies. Images of American Security Bank as an "overweight giant, with arteries clogged by bureaucracy," a "bureaucratic octopus," and a "stumbling bureaucracy" dominated descriptions in the business columns of regional newspapers and of national publications such as the *Wall Street Journal, Businessweek,* and *Fortune.* The *Wall Street Journal* went so far as to conjecture that the effort, on the part of the bank's strategic managers, to change American's bureaucratic culture was "the corporate equivalent of Mao's cultural revolution." In this perspective, the perpetrators of a sluggish bureaucracy were the massive middle ranks of managers in the bank. They were responsible for maintaining a complacent and passive stance toward managing the bank's operations and employees.

Proclaiming to bank employees and to the financial community at large that business as usual—i.e., the banking business of a regulated era—was over, CEO Wedgewood decreed that the "old" culture of the regulated banking period had failed. It had created rule-bound bureaucratic managers who could not make decisions efficiently or seize opportunities for change and innovation. Wedgewood was cited in *Fortune* magazine as saying that

> the existing culture would have preferred to sit back and let me make all those decisions: "Tell us what to do and we'll do it." That was fine but you're not going to develop people that way, you're not going to develop any innovative entrepreneurial approach, and you're not going to develop feedback.[19]

19. To ensure transmission of the new cultural agenda, Wedgewood also circulated tens of thousands of copies (in pamphlet and poster form) of the new cultural manifesto. Although stated as "cultural," the new goals were in fact very concrete ones (such as becoming the number one financial institution and identifying new markets for the bank to enter) that would make the bank more aggressive, competitive, and profitable. All bank employees were expected to

The tool with which managers were to operationalize the new corporate culture was a theory of new management style: "situational leadership,"* which called for abandoning bureaucratic management by rule, substituting it with management by judgment, or instinctual management.

The top leaders of the bank urged middle managers to move away from the stifling, nonentrepreneurial mentality of the culture of rigid rules, embodied in their reliance on the *Standard Procedures Manual (SPM)*. The *SPM* had functioned as a centralized guide on which successful personnel practices in a highly decentralized organizational structure depended. Strategic management claimed that the *SPM* inhibited creative solutions to the burgeoning of personnel problems resulting from the current restructuring of the bank. As Wedgewood stated in an in-house newsletter, "Managers will learn to rely more on their own judgment, within the context of corporate values, and less on the *SPM* and other procedures." The head of corporate personnel concurred in the same newsletter: "No written materials can ever replace the manager's own judgment in managing employees. Managers need to consider each situation individually and determine what's right within the overall corporate culture."

Superimposing the rhetoric of autonomy over an organizational context of uncertainty and contraction, strategic management appealed to managers' professional sensibilities, urging them to act as entrepreneurs and risk takers in order to ensure the bank's survival.[20] Herein lay the ingredi-

---

embrace the new culture, but the middle ranks of managers were its executors; they were to see that the cultural goals were achieved.

20. American Security's attack on the rule-bound individual neatly dovetails the criticism, á la Peters and Waterman, of the "bureaucratic," "organization," or "white-collar" man, so designated by sociologists of the 1950s and 1960s (Mills 1951; Whyte 1956). The culture and personality theorists argued that individuality had been submerged in the dictates of the large corporate organization, characterized as a realm of bureaucratic hierarchy and impersonal manipulation of human relationships rather than things (Margolis 1979; Shorris 1984). Finally, *Businessweek* decisively summarized the fate of the bureaucratically oriented individual. Echoing the current an-

ents of a regime of coercive autonomy. Strategic management was shifting control upward and centralizing functions, processes that removed control, concrete guidelines, and certainty of the future from managers and that undermined their ability to provide significant incentives for working harder. And it was precisely under those conditions that strategic management exhorted lower-level managers to enlarge the discretionary elements of their jobs: to become more innovative and to adopt an aggressive and independent stance toward managing out unproductive employees, in particular, and increasing productivity in general.

Industrial sociologists and others studying the labor process have proposed different conceptualizations of control strategies in the modern workplace. Because they refer almost exclusively to the ways that managers control nonmanagerial workers, these models have limited value for understanding control over managers themselves. Braverman's (1974) notion of the separation of conception and execution, Edwards's (1979) models of direct, technical, and bureaucratic control, and Friedman's (1977) direct control and responsible autonomy strategies have all attempted principally to explain why, how, and when different categories of nonmanagerial workers have been constrained within different social relational and technological contexts across divisions, firms and industries of capitalist society.

To be sure, the notion of bureaucratic control has great applicability to the position of white-collar, professional, and managerial workers. Many workers in these categories are employed by large corporations, in positions where job tasks, compensation, and mobility are governed by a systematized, bureaucratic body of rules and regulations. Bureaucratic systems of control function as much to coordinate the interests of managers and professionals with those of the firm as to

---

tibureaucratic sentiments of popular management theory, *Businessweek* proclaimed that in a "postindustrial," increasingly deregulated business environment, the organization man is dead (21 January 1985).

coordinate the interests of management and production workers.

But as both Edwards (1979) and Osterman (1988) point out, bureaucratic control systems typify very large prosperous firms that have the financial latitude to treat labor as a fixed, stable cost, rather than firms that must continually struggle to increase productivity and pump profits. Bureaucratic control, in sum, is more likely to exist in profitable firms with huge market shares.

Coercive autonomy supersedes bureaucratic control as a strategy of control over managers. It is peculiar to the recent era of corporate restructuring and global competitiveness. Coercive autonomy relies on a postbureaucratic, individualizing language; it explains the current configuration of corporate managerial practices in the competitive, contractive, restructuring era in a way that Edwards's bureaucratic, growth-based model of control cannot. Although it advocates autonomy, it is a highly restricted definition of autonomy in that it directs managers to exercise discretion toward very specific goals of top management. It is, moreover, a coercive model because of the contradictory nature of the demands: managers are to exercise their discretion autonomously, while they are themselves more closely surveyed. Finally, rather than allow managers to focus on the stable and regular execution of tasks (Edwards 1979), the new framework of coercive autonomy pushes managers to focus continually on increasing productivity, initiative, and profitability with the ultimate effect of forcing them to individualize and personalize their management relations.

The new culture of autonomy, calling for flexible, decentralized management methods in the highly restricted context of centralization and cutbacks, obscured the ways in which the historical *organizational legitimacy* of managers' role was being undermined. Throughout the many decades of expansion, the structure of the institution had provided managers an important source of authority and legitimacy. Individual managerial authority was reinforced by the certainty that the organization would pay for effort and by implicit and explicit guarantees of job security. Thus the bureaucratic terms of employment in this large bank virtually assured specific rewards and opportunities to those who met the expectations of their job.

In the new era of competition, strategic management attempted to make middle managers rely much more on *individual legitimacy* or management by judgment. Individual legitimacy would ideally obscure the negative effects of the decrease in predictable rewards and opportunities, as managers individually and personally absorbed the dilemmas of life in an uncertain and capricious organization. Finally, the language of the new culture obscured the effects of corporate contraction on managers' own futures.

Thus organizational and ideological restructuring were the twin pillars of American Security Bank's downsizing. By organizing a series of one-week-long management training seminars, strategic management relayed the principles of the new corporate culture, the new management methods, and the economics of corporate decline to all managers of the bank. Representing a systematic attempt to rebuild management on a grand scale, the seminars brought corporate structural changes to bear on micro-level management practices.

3

Manufacturing Management
Ideology

Trainers to seminar participants:

Any time change is introduced you experience insecurity.
You have to beware of the comfort zone: you're falling into
a network of despair; you need to pull yourself up and
accept change.

Seminar participant to trainers:

I'd rather quit than extract "stretch" from my employees
through your criteria.

Formula presented by trainers:

"SARAH": the stages managers allegedly pass through
when criticized for their management style:

S = shock
A = anger
R = rejection
A = acceptance
H = hope

Management seminars at American Security Bank

In corporation after large American corporation, business
leaders are restructuring their operations to maintain competitiveness. They have placed new objectives such as reducing labor costs—by extracting concessions from professional
and manual workers and increasing worker productivity across

the board (what some call "skimming the fat" from inflated firms)—at the forefront of top management rhetoric and policy.

Corporate leaders now argue for flexibility and change. To set the performance of U.S. corporations back on track, they warn, firms must change their compensation systems for professional and managerial employees (from bureaucratic systems to meritocracies), transform themselves from rigid bureaucracies to flexible, less hierarchical structures, and shift from centralized to decentralized management practices.[1] These new policies radically challenge the terms and conditions of growth-engendered, bureaucratic, and generous employment contracts: the regularized, stable framework of rules governing wages, promotions, and discipline (Edwards 1979).

Transforming corporate cultures also will lead to more competitive corporate performances, according to this new outlook. The idea that corporate cultures can determine the success or failure of large firms has captured the imagination of business observers, academics, and lay persons alike. Peters and Waterman's *In Search of Excellence* (1984) popularized the successful entrepreneurial cultures of such companies as Hewlett-Packard and Procter and Gamble, while studies of the flexible "art of Japanese management" (Athos and Pascale 1981; Ouchi 1981) alerted the public to all that was wrong with rigid American bureaucrats.[2]

1. The proponents of a new corporate ideology include, for example, "progressive" management theorists who analyze both organizational structures and management practices (Naisbett 1982; Kanter 1983; Brandt 1986; Kanter 1987).
2. There has been a significant surge of sociological and organizational research on culture in organizations. Scholarly publications such as the *Administrative Science Quarterly* ("Organizational Culture" 1983), *Organizational Dynamics* ("Organizational Culture" 1983), and the *Journal of Management Studies* ("Organizational Culture and Control" 1986) have devoted entire issues to epistemological and methodological discussions of studying organizational and corporate cultures. Few of these studies have traced the ways in which the recent fascination with culture has shaped organizational practices. They have rather examined how existing cultural symbols and values impede or facilitate organizational objectives, an important,

The business press has taken up the thread, exploring the virtues and disadvantages of evaluating firms from the cultural vantage point. Pascale (1984) extolled the virtues of this perspective, arguing in *Fortune* magazine that management must pay attention to the culture of the firm because a strong culture "supplements formal rules," whereas a weak culture "can make organizational life capricious." In a more skeptical vein, Uttal (1983), also writing in *Fortune*, cast a wary eye on the "corporate culture vultures": consultants who capitalize on their alleged expertise in repairing and redirecting company cultures.

Belief in the significance of culture has become powerful enough that many of its advocates claim that poor, or undermanaged cultures literally can block successful corporate change *(Businessweek,* 14 May 1984; Halloran 1985). Many companies now try to *transform* bureaucratic orientations, to push managers to become more entrepreneurial and to take more risks, in order to overcome the harmful effects of poor cultures.[3] Top managers try to administer new meaning throughout the firm by manipulating company symbols, myths, and history and to overturn complacency by appealing to the pride and loyalty of all company employees.

American Security's strategic management exploited these claims, using the management training seminars to reshape the bank's culture. The issues debated in these seminars are at the heart of the transformation and possible degradation of managerial, professional, and white-collar employment: a necessary transformation, according to the contemporary management theorists, if U.S. industry is to regain its international competitiveness.

The managers who were the subject of this study did not

---

albeit limited, project. See Wilkins's (1989) critical assessment of corporations' misappropriation of the scholarly studies of corporate culture when top managers desperately try to remedy their organizational problems.

3. See Kimberly and Quinn (1984); Berman (1986); *Restructuring Turnaround* (1987); Martin (1988).

have a direct formal role in formulating American Security's restructuring processes, although they were targeted as the principal agents for achieving them. Through the training seminars, strategic management inculcated an ideology of nonbureaucratic, coercive management that would secure the legitimacy for, while obscuring, their restructuring agenda. The seminar trainers gave middle managers the tools to ease out growth-based employment policies and mobility opportunities and to usher in an employment framework shaped by constraint, decline, and an ongoing struggle to achieve profitability. Middle managers were charged with the mission of garnering the consent of employees to the daily, not-so-regularized business of the firm.

If the corporate culture program and the new management methods outlined in Chapter 2 represent the theory of individual judgment or autonomous management, then the seminars and the act of teaching the new program represent the practice, and the trainers the practitioners of individualizing management. In this uniquely collective setting within an otherwise tremendously fragmented social system, middle managers were exposed to the conditions facing other managers and were systematically subjected by the trainers to strategic management's agenda. In addition, the seminar trainers attempted to contain and channel possible resistance to the new managerial agenda by getting managers to discuss their fears of and objections to change and to admit collectively the need for a re-created management. The seminar interactions therefore provide an opportunity to examine the *process* whereby middle managers were targeted as agents and objects of corporate restructuring.

Management Training and Managerial Consent

Management training programs serve, in part, as an arena in which control over, and consent from, management will be gained. Utilizing an elaborate apparatus of in-firm personnel relations, human resources, and management development departments as well as outside consultants, top management in many firms has devoted substantial resources to train managers away from the "point of production" in order to produce and reproduce managerial commitments and ideology.[4]

As early as the 1930s, personnel experts in American industry recognized the importance of special training programs for foremen, above and beyond any "managerial expertise" that could be acquired from experiences on the shop floor (Jacoby 1985). Personnel managers used these programs to reshape foremen's role in a highly volatile political context: top management and personnel specialists believed that foremen's behavior could block, or conversely lead to, unionization of workplaces. "The revival of foremen's training," Jacoby (1985) argues in his study of the emergence of bureaucratic personnel practices, "was industry's plan to use foremen as its first line of defense against unionism" (p. 230).

Training programs attempted to educate foremen about the limitations on their power, encourage them to sell workers on company propaganda, train them in the human relations approach to make them better managers, and bolster their loyalty to the company (Jacoby 1985, pp. 230–231). Thus such programs functioned to regulate the arbitrary exercise of power by foremen and to promote a greater identification between the objectives of foremen and the company. Patten (1968) similarly emphasizes the fact that firms, the War Manpower Commission established during World War II, and YMCA foremen's clubs trained foremen in the area of human relations theory (pp. 110–117).

Management training programs emerged concurrently with a new appreciation for "the mind of management" in the early decades of this century. Corporations, unable to assume a

4. This supplements the common view that managers' allegiance to corporate life is predicated on appropriate socialization (class background, business school training), salary, promotion, and occupational conditions that bind professional or managerial employees to the firms in which they work (Perrow 1986, p. 128).

managerialist orientation, used these training sessions to professionalize and create an "elite" management (Bendix 1956, p. 320). The methods used to reshape the managerial orientation—teaching the human relations approach to managing employees; administering performance ratings of managers through tests and interviews; scheduling weekend, evening, and other regular staff meetings—added up to an agenda of "intensive communication," one aim of which was that managers should manage in a more enlightened and effective fashion.

Some have prescribed training and education programs as a means to gaining managerial-level employees' participation in new corporate goals. One way of smoothing the route to corporate reorganization may be to involve managers in diagnosing current organizational problems. Such organization-wide participation in training programs may increase an overall and coordinated, rather than a departmental or competitive, point of view (Argyris 1955). Furthermore, participation in collective organizational settings is often used to exert top managerial control, contain conflict, and co-opt resistance (Dickson 1981). By organizing group sessions, "top management can establish a framework for participation which allows them to retain effective control" (Dickson 1981, pp. 162–163).

The level of financial commitment made by U.S. firms to management training underscores an ongoing preoccupation with securing managerial commitment to and participation in corporate life. According to a 1986 survey, more firms offer formal training programs to middle managers than to any other occupational group, with the exception of executives (69.5 percent of the firms that responded provide training for executives; 68.9 percent provide training for middle managers; and 61.2 percent of the firms offer training to first-line supervisors; the next highest occupational category to which firms provided training was office/clerical at 50.8 percent). Furthermore, in the firms surveyed, middle managers receive on the average more hours of training (44.2 annually) than any other occupational group (see Gordon 1986b, table 1, p. 49). Another survey concludes that by the year 2000 the average manager will spend eighty-two hours per year in training programs, suggesting that there will be little abatement of this emphasis on training and retraining managers (Fulmer 1986, p. 70).[5]

Indicated by purely economic measures, American Security Bank's seminars represented an extremely significant deployment of resources. The training seminars were organized by an elaborate management development division, set up in 1983 for the sole purpose of administering the managerial turnaround. The management division was staffed by American Security's management-level employees rather than outside management consultants, although outsiders were initially employed to assist in designing the program. At any given time approximately twenty-five managers were teaching the classes; in addition, several managers and supporting staff ran the operation.

The management development division paid a high price to provide a comfortable, even generous setting for the seminars. For the first two years the seminars were nearly always conducted in resort hotels around the state, where all participants stayed for the entire five days.[6] With all expenses paid at vacation-like locations and paid time off from jobs, the seminar week was seen as a privileged break from work.

In structure and timing, the seminars departed radically

5. In addition, more firms reported "management skills training," regardless of occupation, as the principle area in which they provide training; the next highest areas of skills training were very closely related to, if not inseparable from, management skills, such as supervision and communications (Gordon 1986b, p. 54, table 2). This survey was based on a sample of 2,550 firms with a range of 50 to 10,000 or more employees (43.4 percent of the firms had over 2,500 employees; 20.9 percent had over 10,000) (Gordon 1986a, p. 27, table 2).

6. So in addition to the several million poured into the management development division, expenditures for the management turnaround included hotel rental and salaries for all employees while they were away at the seminar.

from the way in which managers had been socialized in the past, changes that indicated a significant organizational measurement of the training. Before the management training program was introduced in 1983, managers received no regular, systematic training as managers in American Security Bank.[7] Although a manager might have attended one of a number of *thematic* classes at some point in his or her career (such as classes in communications, career planning, and leadership or functionally specialized classes such as credit training or use of on-line computer systems), few had attended *occupational* classes that would prepare them for their new role. Furthermore, participation even in thematic programs was inconsistent across the bank. Employees of the bank were frequently promoted into management positions without first undergoing managerial job training. This historical lack of rigorous socialization of managers throws the new agenda for middle managers into even sharper contrast; the new regime represented a major reallocation of organizational resources to re-creating management.

Finally, the use of bank employees to teach the seminars provides testimony to the ideological dimension of the training. Each seminar was run by three trainers, drawn from diverse sectors of the bank. Managers who worked as trainers did so for two years, after which time they returned to the working ranks of management. Coming from diverse organizational locations throughout the bank, the trainers were individuals who had chosen the training position either as a respite from their normal work or because they had been redeployed as a result of restructuring.[8]

7. One could argue that extensive decentralization had really isolated strategic management from the bank's operations. Only as a result of the new, bankwide emphasis on change did strategic management learn fully about the lower ranks of American Security's managers. When they first announced, with great fanfare, that all managers would attend the new program, they anticipated training 9,000 employees; by 1985 CEO Wedgewood proclaimed that 14,000 managers would attend the program by year's end.

8. The trainers I observed, for example, were from the branch

Their personal histories with the bank allowed these in-house trainers to claim that they identified with both the plight of managers and the need for new corporate goals; theoretically they possessed the legitimacy to galvanize others to the mission of the training seminar. The trainers and the seminar attendees were, after all, part of the same big American Security "family."

Many of the seminar trainers evinced what amounted to a religious devotion to strategic management's goals, taking extremely seriously their assignment to incorporate middle managers into the fold of corporate change. As one particularly articulate woman impressed on me, her purpose in working as a management trainer was to spread Wedgewood's message and "give everyone an opportunity to change." Another felt that he had "always been in the role of a change agent, but it was never explicit"; in the role of seminar trainer, he felt that he had found his calling. Even one male trainer who appeared to be somewhat cynical about his "cheerleader" role continually and persuasively turned his acerbic style to the objectives of the seminar, using sarcasm and irreverence to get middle managers to laugh at and criticize themselves.

Despite the sincerity and enthusiasm with which the trainers undertook their mission, their dual structural position imposed a notable tension within the seminar proceedings. On the one hand the trainers were integrated into the personnel management apparatus of the bank; in this sense they were

---

system, systems management, and lending. The trainers were largely a self-selected group. For complex personal and organizational reasons, they had a prior interest in and commitment to working as salespeople for the new corporate culture. Because trainers were ensconced in the seminars for a considerable time, their enthusiasm for the new corporate agenda was not significantly diminished by the "reality factor" other managers faced on their return to the field. Much like the commitments of missionaries in various religious orders, for a two-year period the trainers' work lives were devoted entirely to the seminars. Their enthusiasm was, however, occasionally strained by the participants' antagonism.

the agents of strategic management's agenda. On the other hand, their insider status occasionally made them more vulnerable to managers' hostility. Their common position as managers in the bank increased their empathy with middle managers, often leading them to accept passively the full brunt of managers' criticisms about the organizational changes taking place.

Their struggle to reconcile these two facets of their position, to make sense of the hostility showered on them by seminar participants, without, for the most part, condemning those participants, was often painfully apparent. At several very awkward moments in the seminars, the trainers truly lacked answers for the concerns participants were raising. However, this did not stop the trainers from otherwise maintaining a very consistent approach in steering and controlling group discussions.[9]

Inside the Management Seminars: Organization and Politics

My position at a table with the trainers in the back of the seminar room gave me a comprehensive view of the entire seminar proceedings. In contrast, only a handful of participants could see us. Those attending the seminar sat at a U-shaped arrangement of tables: facing each other around the U, the fifteen to twenty-five participants were fully visible to one another. The very formal, even lavish, environment (all the tables had floor-length skirted tablecloths; each place setting had an elegant name card facing outward for all to see; large pitchers of ice water were placed every few feet along the table; and every position had a pile of literature—fat binders full of seminar information—along with pens and pencils imprinted with the company logo) contributed to a

9. This type of "processual containment" on the part of the trainers is consistent with the seminar processes described by Jacoby (1985, p. 229) and Hochschild (1983, chap. 6).

sense of important purpose. Indeed, we were all about to em-
bark on the very serious and collective endeavor of reconstructing management.

American Security's management seminars shared many
characteristics of human potential courses; the "take responsibility for your own actions" ethos, so dominant in the human potential movement, enhanced the objective of individualizing management.[10] Managers participated extensively,
as the trainers encouraged them to examine and discuss their
feelings about the many changes confronting them. Although
there was a high tolerance for "sharing" one's feelings, however, the range of topics and the tone in which they were discussed were closely managed by the seminar trainers.

The trainers walked the participants through a number of
curriculum modules and attempted to delimit carefully the
directions in which discussions could move. The objectives of
the seminar included describing the theory behind the newly
instituted performance planning, coaching, and evaluation
system (PPCE),* and discussing situational leadership and the
new corporate culture, otherwise known as "Vision, Values,
and Strategy."

Techniques to regularize management pervaded all aspects of the seminar and its preparation. The standardization
of course materials and curriculum created a coherent and
professional image of the project at hand. Visual devices such
as charts, graphs, and poster-size illustrations were hung
around the conference room. Each class member received

10. Recently there has been furor over the introduction of human
potential approaches into the workplace. The *New York Times* reported an increase of lawsuits by employees who feel they have been
unduly pressured to participate in activities, such as self-exploration
techniques and group therapy, that conflict with their personal or
religious values. These activities have been organized toward the
goal of increasing workplace productivity. One man who worked for
an auto dealership contended, for example, that the teaching of "New
Age Thinking to Increase Dealership Profitability" was "inimical to
his religious views" (*New York Times*, 17 April 1987). American Security's human potential side was comparatively toned down.

reams of written material mass-produced for the seminars by the bank's management development division. Consisting of books explaining the use of the PPCE, salary administration, and how to be a career counselor to one's employees, the material also included a number of articles on corporate culture, change, and resistance to change from such business publications as the *Harvard Business Review.*

Before attending the seminar each manager engaged in a self-monitoring exercise by filling out a "leadership practices inventory" (LPI) and administering this same inventory to his or her employees. The inventory assessed how good a leader each manager was from the perspective of both the manager and the people he or she managed. (Inventory items asked whether they managed conflict or change well and whether or not they were good decision makers.) The manager submitted all the inventories to the management development staff, who tallied up the results. The trainers distributed computerized tabulations of each manager's leadership skills, results that were later used to analyze and suggest improvements for the manager's performance.[11]

The trainers began by having participants state their names and what they wanted to gain from the seminar. Managers' statements simultaneously reflected their uneasiness about the

11. Since the *N* size of the inventory respondents was generally quite small (most of the inventories ranged from three to six responses) the inventory probably had a function other than to provide a meaningful measurement of a manager's managing skills. Zuboff's work may inadvertently be helpful for understanding the more implicit and coercive function of such tests. Zuboff (1985) touts the leveling effects of coordinating knowledge of production processes between managerial and nonmanagerial workers. She argues that engaging both workers and supervisors in data generation and evaluation (rather than mystifying the process by leaving it in the hands of managers) makes them "brethren in the data" rather than perpetuates unnecessary relations of power and hierarchy (p. 134). As workers and managers become "brethren" in the act of evaluating managers, one basis of managerial authority—ability to assert the managerial prerogative about knowing what it takes to manage effectively—diminishes greatly. This could be one form of what Blau and Schoenherr (1971) call "insidious control."

very meaning of the managerial role in the context of the bank's crisis and expressed their interest in viable management guidelines. Comments ranged from "I want to learn how to be a good people manager," "I need to learn hands-off managing," and "I want to learn how to get good people to work harder when they don't want to" to "I'm trying to decide whether or not I even want to be a manager," and "I need to learn to cope with the PPCE."[12]

The trainers then proceeded with a presentation that showed how the bank's changes were related to the crisis in the banking industry. Always careful to emphasize the factors external to the firm that were creating a need for a new managerial orientation, the trainers showed the "big picture"—the turbulent environmental and financial conditions facing the bank—and its effects on working conditions in the office and on the shop floor. The discussion of the bank's financial and organizational difficulties, market factors in particular, parallels the "exposure strategy" cited by Whalley (1986) in his study of engineers. Firms encouraged a "managerialist" orientation by exposing their engineering employees to financial and organizational information about the company's competitive situation (p. 227). Presumably exposure compels employees—professional or managerial—to identify with and work to achieve profitability objectives.

Starting with the principles of the new corporate culture captured in the program of Vision, Values, and Strategies, the trainers demonstrated how the larger direction and profitability of the bank directly affected and were affected by what went on in the bank's many divisions, offices, and branches. They further argued that they could offer concrete tools to

12. One indication that strategic management had successfully and informally disseminated the fact that managers were to be critically evaluated for the way they used the PPCE came from the management development division. In an interview, one trainer informed me that the division had been "bombarded with phone calls" requesting information about proper use of the PPCE, as managers throughout the bank realized they would be held accountable for and through the PPCE system.

enable managers to make a positive contribution to the bank's larger direction.

The trainers introduced the Performance Planning, Coaching, and Evaluation (PPCE) procedure as the mechanism linking corporate strategic plans to daily work processes at all levels of the bank. The procedure would allow middle managers to translate top management's plans for a leaner, more entrepreneurial, nonbureaucratic organization into concrete personnel and employment policies. As one trainer noted, discussing a chart that showed the relationship between corporate business plans and the "action plans" of individual managers, the PPCE "holds this whole scheme together."

Throughout the seminar exercises, managers demonstrated a good understanding of the big picture and agreed with the general need for greater productivity to improve the financial health of the corporation. The consensus emerged that to rectify the current crisis, action was necessary at all levels of the corporation. This consensus is the axis of intramanagement unity, representing the convergence of middle and strategic management interests.

But another consensus emerged, one that united *middle* managers but separated them from strategic management. While lower-level managers agreed with strategic management's agenda for achieving larger profitability objectives, they diverged from that agenda over the methods by which those objectives could be achieved. Although corporate restructuring created very different pressures for different groups of managers, these managers nevertheless agreed that the new managerial orientation would undermine rather than promote long-term consent to the restructuring process; they felt that their ability to elicit productive work behavior was threatened by what they perceived as a skewed definition of entrepreneurialism and an arbitrary set of management methodologies.

Middle managers anticipated heightened politicization resulting from the new emphasis on using individual managerial judgment to push through a new productivity program.

In the context of contraction and the decline of organization-wide mechanisms of control, the arbitrary management schemes and the new definition of management on which they were based would weaken bases for managerial authority. The trainers countered these concerns by reinterpreting the organizational politics of corporate restructuring as neutral organizational problems *caused* by individual psychological maladjustment, and to be *solved* by individual managerial judgment.

Extracting Greater Effort: Minimum Job Requirements

Recent theories of corporate structure have blamed lack of productivity and innovation in large corporations on too great a dependence on centralized, bureaucratic rules. Thus some have argued for replacing strictly bureaucratic organization with less hierarchical, more fluid structures which would facilitate decentralized, innovative management action (cf. Kanter's [1983] discussion of the "integrative" corporation). American Security Bank imported elements of this critique of bureaucratic behavior into the new management platform. One attempt to redress the ills of bureaucracy consisted of weaning managers and employees from the allegedly binding and stultifying job descriptions on which positions had historically been based.

Emphasis on merely satisfactory job performance, according to the seminar trainers, was a legacy of a profitable, complacent banking environment. Managers who did not look for ways to wring more out of the jobs and the people they managed were encouraging mediocrity. Thus managers should look for ways to "raise the bar"*: to upgrade *jobs* by raising the "minimum job requirements" (MJRs)* for positions. In so doing managers could become innovators in their own units. The trainers argued that middle managers should reorient their thinking away from bureaucratically constricting, standardized job descriptions based on position and focus instead on increasing results in order to contribute to improved corpo-

rate performance. This they would do by setting "stretch objectives"*: upgrading *people* by pushing them to achieve even
higher levels of output.[13] In lieu of specific recommendations
for upgrading jobs and jobholders, the seminar trainers continually advocated leaving managers alone to upgrade through
vigorous and flexible use of management judgment.

The trainers informed me, before "class" began, that the
discussions of MJRs were always the most difficult modules
of the seminars, because managers held so much "irrational
resistance" toward this fundamental change in their orientation to managing. This precaution heightened my anticipa-
tion of the module devoted to the MJR. What was it about
this topic that could unnerve the trainers so much that they
would warn me about it beforehand? Why were middle managers so protective of "across the board" or organizationally
consistent MJRs?

The discussions of minimum requirements for a job demonstrate why American Security's managers held a quite rational resistance to the demise of a bureaucratic framework
for managing. From middle managers' perspective, companywide standardized job expectations were important for
regularizing their evaluations of employees' performance. The
loss of such standards connoted a level of chaos that would
undermine the new responsibilities with which these managers were saddled. Yet in the seminars the trainers insisted
that the bank, in its current process of change, could no longer
come up with positional levels appropriate for the entire corporation. Managers must use their own judgment instead and
take responsibility for determining new and higher job expectations.

After introducing the idea that managers should deemphasize minimum job requirements and emphasize increased results, one of the trainers attempted to neutralize

13. In essence managers were being asked to raise both bottom-
line productivity levels for merely satisfactory job performance and
the productivity levels that would qualify employees for merit raises.
This was part of the "managing up" program.

the politics of upgrading jobs and individuals. Rather than discuss MJRs as an important benchmark by which managers could consistently evaluate employees, this trainer attempted to get managers to think of MJRs as something merely psychological. Calling MJRs "only a tool, only a consideration in the thought process," she anticipated managers' reluctance to abandon a more centralized framework for managing, acknowledging in a sympathetic voice that "many of you will find it hard to come up with positional MJRs." She went on to place the onus on managers, however, saying "You as manager need to go through the thought process, figure out what you need. There are very few positions in the corporation for which we can come up with across-the-board MJRs."

She admonished the seminar participants not to expect centralized guidelines in measuring employee performance. Insisting that standardized job requirements were inappropriate for a firm as diverse and changing as rapidly as American Security, this trainer suggested that they were, in fact, the true impediments to productive management; reworking productivity standards through the appropriate thought process was the sign of the truly entrepreneurial manager.

Another trainer hinted at the real purpose behind "de-emphasizing" MJRs; he repeated the charge that standardized expectations of employees block innovation and productivity. His approach is telling, for it recasts the productivity problem as a problem of individuals and their psychological propensities. "Let's think about human nature," he argued. "If we just had MJRs, why would people work any harder than just the minimum?"

One trainer, named Kathryn, reiterated that managers should be "raising the bar" (or minimums) of as many jobs as they could. Dave, a seminar participant, argued against managers' role in utilizing personal judgment to shift the boundaries of productivity in this way: "If we don't have a standard, we can't do this." Kathryn insisted that in fact Dave did have a standard—his managerial judgment. Management judgment simply did not carry weight with Dave, however.

Thinking ahead to his work situation, Dave touched on the contradiction between the agenda of the seminar (to get managers to increase productivity and to slim down the corporation in a context of contraction and declining rewards) and the tools being offered to managers to achieve that agenda. He insisted that strategic management should execute the new corporate agenda more directly by selling assets and closing unprofitable units, arguing that middle managers did not have the means to manage effectively by individual judgment. To Kathryn's claim that he possessed a valid standard, Dave replied, "No, I don't, but the corporation does. And this is leading to change and downgrading. We cannot manage these processes without a corporate standard."

Middle managers quickly caught on to what it meant in practice to deemphasize standardized job descriptions in the service of higher productivity levels. Helen argued that if everyone in her unit were told that they had different and fluctuating MJRs, she could say goodby to any possibilities for increasing productivity. Her employees would constantly be at Employee Relations (an employee/management mediating unit within the bank) to force greater consistency in evaluation procedures. Other participants jumped into this discussion, with Mavis asserting that "If there are different MJRs for fourteen different people in similar jobs, there is going to be trouble." A trainer intervened to redirect what had become a very contentious drift, arguing that raising job minimums to different levels for different individuals was a very natural task, simply part of a thought process in which managers logically connected individual job performance with the larger profitability objectives of the firm.[14] "We may be get-

14. This individualizing tendency was startlingly evident in an unrelated discussion about ranking individual employees. Admonishing managers for their reluctance to give raises and promotions by frankly comparing each and every employee, Kathryn stated, "You simply can't make a commitment [to employees about achieving merit increases in pay]. You articulate this as stretch; *you'll say something very different to every employee* based on their maturity [emphasis added]."

ting off on a tangent. The key is that managers must go through
the thought process of knowing what you need for business
goals and articulate these minimums to employees. It's a tool."

The trainers' behavior during discussions of MJRs and objectives visibly expressed their discomfort at being the objects of managers' antagonism. They walked nervously around
the room, they more frequently interrupted discussions among
participants, and they called for unscheduled break intervals
at the peaks of heated discussions.

Trainers also used dismissive statements, such as "We may
be getting off on a tangent" or "That's an excellent point and
I'd like to save that for a future discussion" to defuse "hot
points" during the seminars. But this marginalizing tactic did
not deter Helen from insisting that concepts such as "thought
process" and "individual judgment" were vague and of little
help. The trainers might extol the virtues of management theory, claiming it provided an orderly and rational means of
gaining greater worker effort, but the difficulty of managing
the politics of a speedup were clear to Helen. Her concern,
she argued, was not with abstractions and theory, but with
"fairness and consistency. The practicality [of managing up
employees' performance] is, you'd better know what you're
doing."

The seminar trainers used the language of thought process
to promote a framework of individual, innovative managerial
action, at the same time playing down the negative implications of the new framework. The language allowed the trainers to dilute the significance of both the pressure on middle
managers to increase productivity and the lack of centralized
guidelines for doing so. In the framework of individualized
responsibility, MJRs were no longer a set of guidelines for
evaluating job performance: they were no more than an element of the thought process through which managers had to
go to increase productivity.

Managers were not agents of a speedup of their employees'
work: their role in increasing results was merely part of a
thought process in which working to increase productivity

steadily was a normal task, to be rationally incorporated into a manager's everyday job. The trainers minimized the import of "raising the bar" by expressing surprise and scoffing at the disturbed responses of the seminar participants. Recasting the political problems of consent and cooperation as simple individual problems, the trainers insinuated that any rational manager should be able to resolve the "minor" conflicts of organizational change.

At the same time, the insistent focus on managerial judgment to increase productivity formalized strategic management's agenda to individualize the responsibility of corporate change. As managers repeatedly voiced their dissent to having to manage each individual employee with less centralized guidance, they met even greater insistence that they were to use situational leadership to obtain higher performance levels from all employees.

In response to managers' apprehensions about the new emphasis on increasing results, one of the trainers cavalierly suggested that managers should simply write in (on employee performance evaluations) as much stretch as possible. After a manager carefully considers all aspects of a position and an employee's capabilities, that manager should "take risks" to "encourage workers to increase output": the trainer asked, "Shouldn't we raise the bar? Don't we ask more of them?" Sandy, a branch manager concerned about the disruptive aspects of both the random application of high stretch levels and the sudden transition from rewards for efforts and seniority to rewards for results, was very agitated as she asked, "How do you arbitrarily raise the bar for someone who has worked with the bank for fifteen years?" The trainer gave a response that reflected the individualizing thrust of situational leadership: "You know management isn't easy. You've got to use J. You need to get involved in the process. *We* can't give you a cookbook."

The managers attending the seminars did not disagree with the need to find more effective ways of managing, but they did protest the impact that these particular methods would have on managerial effectiveness and legitimacy. Chris's response further illuminates middle managers' dilemma over the demise of more standardized guidelines in this organizational context. Chris was responsible for over eighty indirect reports in an area management group in the retail division. She was an extremely accomplished employee and had received the bank's prestigious "golden pin of merit" (an award given out by the corporate personnel department for outstanding performance); at the end of the week-long seminar her fellow participants voted her "best manager" of their class. Presumably an ideal manager from the perspective of top management, Chris expressed her agreement throughout the seminar for many of top management's goals. But she was also quite articulate about her differences with certain aspects of those goals.

After a particularly long and antagonistic discussion of the process of raising the bar and deemphasizing minimum job requirements in which she urged that managers not penalize employees for managerial misjudgment, Chris attempted to sum up the basis of the group's opposition to the methodologies presented by the trainers: "I think we felt threatened when you said to *take away* the minimum job requirements. You're taking away one of our important measuring tools." Her comment seemed to embolden Ralph, who earlier had expressed anger when the trainers denied the importance of bureaucratic standards. He interjected, "You got my back up over the terminology change. Different areas have different needs and standards. When you admit the importance of MJRs I don't get bent out of shape. I'm going to go back and do things exactly the same way I have been." Judging by the rather defiant murmur that followed his words, this opinion was shared by others as well.

Managing Structural Change

Managers' fears were exacerbated similarly when they were confronted with the demand to increase productivity and set new objectives in the context of "nonnegotiable" changes*:

loss of personnel and funding and possible workplace closure. These structural transformations complicated managers' role in pressuring employees for greater work effort. And the language and management method of individualization failed to obscure the exploitative nature of the changes taking place, on which individual managerial legitimacy had little bearing.

Barry, for example, had comanaged a branch for several years in the position of branch administrative officer. He insisted that a key problem from his perspective lay in getting his employees to stretch (to become more productive) when the branches were undergoing staff reductions. Barbara, another branch manager, articulately summed up the contradiction inherent in demanding stretch in a context of diminishing resources:

> As managers we're told to cut staff; we're told to turn our tellers and ourselves into quality salespeople; and as managers we are supposed to increase our supervision and general productivity. Branch managers are really figureheads in terms of authority, yet we're under all this pressure: there is not really very much we can do.

These pressures similarly affected Rose, who managed fourteen loan collection officers in the Southern California area. As the loan function was being centralized, her loan officers couldn't "really give quality customer service. We don't have the expertise or tools anymore to give informed answers to customer questions." Further under the gun because her unit was responsible for loan collection at precisely the time that the bank was facing unprecedented loan defaults, Rose expressed great frustration over the fact that at her previous branch loan officers had been pushed to "sell paper": to lend out money as rapidly as possible.

Rose's lack of control over the way functional changes affected the jobs of her loan officers undermined her ability to understand existing productivity objectives, quite apart from formulating new and higher ones. The transformation of this function held other implications for Rose's job, because an increase in customer complaints (due to confusion over the new organization of the loan process) appeared on her PPCE as one negative measurement of her ability to "manage change." When Rose expressed a great deal of anger about the bank's continuing to make loans when its loan losses were beginning to look severe, Kathryn suggested that Rose should seek innovative ways of facing the managerial challenge and recommended that Rose ask herself "What can *I* do to help this situation?" This individualistic recommendation triggered a long and heated discussion about managers' actual lack of control over their work situations.

Managers were supposed to manage employees in a context of extreme organizational uncertainty as the structure, labor process, and function of divisions changed unevenly throughout the bank. When managers raised concerns about managing uncertainty, they were given individualizing mechanisms for coping.[15] Middle managers frequently lamented the fact that they were kept in the dark about pending corporate changes. Kathryn, one of the trainers, responded that managers should not reveal their ignorance about the corporate restructuring process to their employees. Good managers, she argued, were opaque and would maintain individual legitimacy by concealing the inadequacy of their knowledge about the decline of the organization.

> Managers should not be transparent. If a manager has to make a decision and it is difficult—for example, if you're involved in a major centralization of functions, or redeployment—when you're communicating these changes to the employee, you should not be transparent.

15. Indeed, when one woman manager questioned why managers were not told about pending change, a trainer reversed the challenge, his patronizing tone conveying the distinct impression that her wish to know reflected a deep personality flaw: "The really important thing is, Why is this an important issue to you?"

You don't want to be saying "I don't really understand why the company wants us to do this, but . . ."

Helen, who managed a group of data-entry workers, expressed her frustration with this cryptic approach to managing change. One of the objectives on her PPCE on which *she* would be evaluated was to increase the productivity of her workers. But rumors were sweeping through her unit that some of these positions were going to be eliminated. Her work group had subsequently been severely demotivated *(sic)* and she had been unable to justify stretching on other than purely coercive terms ("no stretching, no jobs"). Thus what was transparent in her position was her lack of control over and knowledge about the fate of the unit and her inability to conceal the exploitative aspects of demands for a greater contribution to the firm.

Her workers plied her with questions about their future. She told her seminar colleagues, "If I don't know why something is happening, I will say I just don't understand." She felt that this bluntness, although it was a kind of manipulation, would lend her far more credibility in the managing process. Kathryn retorted, "What is your gut feeling? Use the Big J; be proactive; think ahead and be more managing and instrumental." Helen responded, "I will try to find out what's happening, but I am often unable to do so."

Kathryn refused to admit any larger organizational responsibility for managers' dilemmas, continuing instead to pin responsibility for managing conflict and change squarely to the shoulders of middle managers. She expressed an extreme version of the individualist argument. "You're responsible for your own fate," she claimed.

The corporation may own your job but you own your career. You have to try to manage the situation. If employees think they can see through you, you won't get a commitment from them. The onus is on managers. Managers have to write the PPCEs; you have to be taken seriously. Managers have to support top management. You have to be genuine. We don't want "just compliance" from managers.

Sandy contended that this managerial approach to change was simply irrelevant to her case: her employees discovered their branch was closing only when some workers came by to place a bid on the reconstruction of their building. As one single manager, Sandy rejected the idea that her legitimacy would justify, much less obscure, this type of corporate change.

In the course of the seminar no definitive solutions were given for achieving significantly higher productivity levels when employees and managers were unsure of their occupational outcomes and when managers, with fewer personnel and budgetary resources, lacked legitimate grounds for making employees work harder. When seminar participants persisted in pushing harder to know how they were to extract more from employees with fewer resources and guidelines, the trainers continually redirected responsibility for the solution back onto the managers. As one trainer stated, "We used to use the *SPM* as a source for all dos and don'ts. But times have changed. We can't only follow rules; we have to ask ourselves: Does this make sense?"

Nor were managers satisfied that genuinely autonomous exercise of their judgment was unambiguously sanctioned by top management. Managing out looked like a murky process to middle managers, because the consequences of pushing workers to unreasonable limits to increase productivity were clear. If a manager had not clarified and documented every aspect of a work situation to the employee but had nevertheless fired or downgraded him or her, the employee might feel that he or she had been misled and later sue the bank—a turn of events for which the manager would ultimately be held responsible.

Several discussions centered on the procedures and implications of managing out. The trainers used "case studies" to teach managers how to identify and deal with poor performers. Many managers, however, were concerned about the ambiguities of this process. Andy had managed eight people in a branch in the Los Angeles area for seven years. He had been told that if a manager used language such as "might terminate" in an employee's PPCE, and a labor board brought a case against the bank for wrongful termination, "the judge might highlight the 'might' and inquire what the alternatives were. It would shore up the employee's case against the manager."

The sensitive nature of managers' position in managing up or out was further driven home by Ken, who had managed four lawyers in the bank's litigation department for three years. As an older man, Ken had a perspective on the firm's legal position gained from many years of private practice outside the bank and from his location in the administrative inner sanctum of the bank. Ken was adamant; once a promise to an employee had been violated, he warned, a manager should anticipate legal action taken by that employee. "You're in a litigation context," he argued, "once a major screwup has happened in personnel policy."

In one module of the seminar, trainers and participants discussed a case study of a female employee who brought a discrimination suit against American Bank. The intention of the discussion was to ascertain who and what had been responsible for bringing on the suit. Tom, one of the trainers, argued that the fault lay with the manager: "Lack of communication is the root cause of the problem. She can file a discrimination suit—but what happens to American Bank when a suit is filed? It gives the corporation a bad image. *Managers should be talking to employees who feel discriminated against.*" Managers would be directly evaluated, on their PPCEs, on how well they used their judgment in avoiding these negative scenarios.

Almost without fail, managers responded with confusion and frustration to trainers' claims that managers must exercise discretion and judgment in dealing with employees. As one participant wryly noted, "We're given discretion about disciplinary action, but if I follow exactly what I want, the bank may be sued. I constantly must look for advice. My *employees* know the SPM—they would be great managers." At which point one of the trainers redirected the discussion: "Let's keep this question in mind. I hope we can answer this during the week. We have to remember the Big J. Your judgment: Can I do this or can't I?" Every so often the contradictions inherent in the Big J would bubble to the surface. When Diane questioned how a manager was to suspend a so-called poor performer, the trainers went to such lengths to caution her that she burst out, "What happened to my judgment as a manager? Suddenly I can't do anything unless I ask seventeen people before I send someone home."

Behind the concerns that managers had about increasing output was the very serious problem of defining output and productivity rates in production contexts that defied easy codification and quantification; this problem characterized many of the work sites within this bank, and of course, many work sites within firms and industries in a "postindustrial" or service-based economy. The fact that managers were being asked to increase productivity when minimal standardized guidelines existed for many jobs in the first place led to a good deal of confusion and frustration, expressed both in the training seminars and in interviews.

Ken, the corporate attorney mentioned above, was furious about the individualizing bias and the vague standards for productivity, in which all responsibility for productivity was deemed to be the middle manager's. When his seminar group was shown a diagram illustrating how each manager was supposed to increase the output of his or her department by getting every employee to stretch, he exclaimed, "How does this get affected if the input is inadequate? When I don't have enough people I cannot increase output."

Trainers insisted that output was the responsibility of the manager. Bill equated output with a manager's efforts, asserting that employees will strive to accomplish what they think the boss wants: "It's the manager who doesn't see the environment properly, who doesn't expect enough stretch, who doesn't give challenging enough assignments." The trainers referred to managers who would not get their employees to stretch as deadwood, old-timers who resisted change. Despite this condemnation, Diane blurted out in frustration that she would rather quit than extract stretch from her employees through the criteria proposed by the trainers.

The individualizing thrust was similarly expressed whenever seminar participants attempted to direct discussion of the current profitability crisis toward strategic management. When trainers admonished them for middle managerial shortsightedness and for being more self-centered than firm-centered, seminar participants in turn challenged the firm's historical stress on what they called "corporate" as distinct from "moral" values and questioned whether top management was "being honest" about the root causes of the current dilemma.

The trainers trivialized dissenting individuals' efforts by forcing participants to "own" their contesting statements as mere personal opinions, again neutralizing the political issues of organizational restructuring by characterizing the dissenters as organizational miscreants. Anytime participants questioned the incompatibility between the human needs of people who worked in the corporation and the needs of profit making, trainers dismissed the seriousness of the conflicts and reduced them to "breakdowns" in managers' communication of the goals of the corporation to individuals.

Managers anticipated many contradictory consequences from having to increase productivity and reduce personnel just as standardized measures to implement this ambitious agenda were disappearing. Thus intramanagement conflict crystallized in a struggle over the very meaning and function of bureaucracy. As strategic management pushed the ideological critique of managerial bureaucrats, middle managers asserted their case for centralized, bureaucratic criteria in order to implement the new agenda. The seminars became a site of struggle over the terms of management: managers challenged the new definition of entrepreneurial management in an environment of contraction and challenged the ways in which they were supposed to extract greater effort from those they managed.

Conclusion

Do the American Security Bank seminar proceedings mirror a battle taking place across the ranks of American corporate management, a struggle over the theory of management and over corporate management practices? Other examples support the claim that corporations use cultural programs to position managers as objects and agents of corporate change in this current era of industrial restructuring. These examples also point to high levels of conflict within management over the new norms contained in cultural platforms.

The very terminology of reporting in business publications suggests a cultural onslaught against middle levels of management, a trend not confined to information, financial, or service industries. One of the most well-publicized efforts deliberately to transform a corporate culture has been that of General Motors Corporation. Changing its culture was a tactical move in a long-term effort to "reinvigorate" the company's business standing (*Businessweek*, 7 April 1986). In its "corporate civil war" (presumably the equivalent of American Security's "cultural revolution"), the auto firm cracked down on a perceived "culture of complacency" and the ethos that permeated what chief executive officer Roger Smith called the "frozen middle" of management. Thawing out that frozen middle by eliminating bureaucratic layers of managers—eliminating one-quarter of its managerial work force by 1990, to be precise—was one of the central aims of GM's corporate culture program (*Fortune*, 10 November 1986).

A similar effort was undertaken by the Ford Motor Company. The firm administered tests of managerial style and culture in workshops for managers; 76 percent of those tested were classified as "noncreative types," too willing to accept authority (*Wall Street Journal*, 3 December 1985). One observer declared the 1980s the "decade of the cultural revolution" after American Telephone and Telegraph adopted a program for changing its company culture during its breakup (Turnstall 1986). Prechel's (1986) study of a corporate cultural change in a large steel company yields conclusions much like those drawn in this chapter: the emphasis on changing cultures can be a transitional strategy of almost last resort for top managements in declining and restructuring industries. As Ray (1986) suggests, the arena of culture may constitute the last frontier of control for corporate top management.[16]

The growing attention paid to management ideology and culture reflects a greater preoccupation with reshaping the values of American management to make managers willing ushers of corporate change. But in important ways these new management philosophies obscure organizational changes that undermine rather than promote managers' ability to act as agents of change.[17]

16. When Pacific Bell (California) decided to change its company culture it invested $30 million in "leadership development training" sessions (called Krone training after the management consultant who designed it), which all 67,000 of its employees would attend. Many employees filed complaints about the training, claiming that they were coerced into attending. Local media discovered that a major purpose of the training was to forge new, nonconflictual relations with the Communications Workers of America (representing approximately two-thirds of the PacBell work force) (*San Francisco Chronicle*, 23 March 1987; 27 March 1987).

17. Ray (1989) similarly emphasizes this function of the recent preoccupation with corporate cultures. For Ray, transforming the corporate culture represents an attempt to "socially reskill" managers so that they will work harder, interpersonally, to get employees to swing their efforts to the larger good of the corporation. That was certainly one goal of American Security Bank's corporate culture agenda. However, the *particular* content of these new ideologies for middle managers must be stressed: the cultural themes revolve around the entrepreneurial manager, who in his or her everyday management practices will take an active role in downsizing the ranks of corporate employees (managerial and nonmanagerial) and will forge ahead to a new, leaner corporate America.

The conflicts taking place in the seminars are significant insofar as they reflect a lack of unity about the means and ends of the new corporate restructuring agenda. But the seminar proceedings also fueled and heightened antistrategic politics. Managers regularly expressed their skepticism about the aims of strategic management as they were transmitted in the seminar. If anything, the seminar heightened their awareness of the contradictions in the new orientation. Frank Cosgrove stated that top management was charging middle managers with reducing the bank's personnel but was hiding this mission behind depoliticized and optimistic language and "opaque" management. In his opinion, strategic management was asking middle management to manage by Theory X under the pretense that it was using Theory Y. In other words, managers were supposed to appear enlightened (the Theory Y manager) yet act in a more coercive fashion (the Theory X manager).[18] One branch manager could find no better term for the management philosophies, presented in the seminar and in the array of management literature distributed throughout the bank, than "brainwashing."

The theorists of new management philosophies have presented an ideal picture of nonhierarchical participatory corporate structures. They focus almost exclusively on the drawbacks of bureaucracy and criticize managers for preserving bureaucratic rigidity. They minimize or ignore, however, the degree to which bureaucratic norms provide an important source of consent to objectives corporate America is under so much pressure to achieve: such norms ensure rewards and regularize relations within the workplace. Under conditions of organizational contraction, centralization, and the elimination of monetary or mobility incentives, managers may view bureaucratic norms as one of the few sources of their ability to manage. Managers' demand that certain rules be left intact does not necessarily indicate organizational conservatism (al-

18. Cosgrove was referring to McGregor's (1960) model of the two most prevalent managerial styles.

though certainly in some cases it may): rather, as American Security Bank's middle managers recognized, their ability to secure consent and gain greater productivity levels depends to some degree on regularized reward and feedback procedures.

The current focus on controlling managers through corporate culture and ideological reform parallels attempts through the scientific management movement to control lower-level production and clerical workers. Whereas scientific management programs break down and colonize the physical movements of lower-level workers, corporate culture agendas attempt to specify the precise content and meaning of middle managers' social relations.

Striving to control employees through cultural mechanisms, however, may be limited in the same way that scientific management was limited in its applications to lower levels of workers (Edwards 1979, pp. 97–104). The theory of cultural control frequently ignores such variables as the historical and organizational context of the workplace, the complex and unequal relations between different strata of management, and the relations between managers and those they manage. This theory also ignores the fact that cultures emerge from the actual structures of organizations and work processes; deliberate attempts to transform culture from the top down and at a purely symbolic level may thus face serious obstacles (Ouchi and Wilkins 1985, p. 476). The vibrant entrepreneurial cultures that the new management theorists wish to create may be most typical in expanding, growth-based firms and may not be replicable in firms facing serious profitability pressures.

Middle managers' responses to change at American Security can best be explained by the particular organizational context in which they were to exercise the new managerial agenda. Calling for entrepreneurialism, flexibility, and heightened use of discretion, the new agenda simultaneously delimited what an entrepreneur was, how his or her tasks should be executed, and the repercussions of failing to exercise discretion in a way that served the corporation's purposes. In short, the platform of the new corporate culture substituted coercive, individualized responsibility for the autonomy and flexibility of the entrepreneur.

Furthermore, in the view of middle managers, strategic management's definition of arbitrarily inflated productivity standards, opaque management, and flexibility were inviable and potentially costly to the firm. Located at the intersection between the global changes of the firm and the effects of these changes in the bank's various work sites, managers predicted that the new methods would fail. The success of the program depended on exploiting managers' individual legitimacy, but the program itself undermined the legitimacy they needed to achieve corporate objectives.

Ralph, a manager, commented on the difficulties of acting like entrepreneurs and innovators in a context that continually undermined legitimacy, authority, and autonomous action. "We're encouraged to develop entrepreneurship; we're given visions, values, and strategy. But they're unfocused in relation to what managers have to do. When it conflicts with reality it's a problem." And insofar as the seminars were the site of strategic management's attempts to produce new managerial standards that contradicted the realities managers faced every day, the seminars became the site of struggle over the very definition of entrepreneurial behavior and over the terms by which managers were to extract greater effort from employees.

4

Managing in
the Corporate Interest

By resisting the directive to manage out new categories of poor performers, middle managers rejected the means top management identified as best serving the corporate interest. The next three chapters describe that resistance and analyze why middle managers refused to act as agents of restructuring along the lines mandated by strategic management.

Sociologists and organizational researchers have typically studied management action from one of two reigning orthodoxies. The "postclass" model of employment conditions and relations of authority presumes harmonious intramanagement relations (a result of the coordination of management and professional interests with the objectives of the firm), autonomous work conditions, and employment conditions untouched by unemployment or decline (Bell 1973). An implicit model of corporate organization, based on growth, decentralization, and certainty of environment (Chandler 1962), bolsters such presumptions. In this framework, different groups in industrial society transcend their conflicting class relations.[1]

---

1. In a modernization version of this thesis, Kerr (1964) argues that in a mature industrialized society managers and managed will

The postclass view of American society is closely related to a corresponding sociological tradition of management studies: research on organizational behavior.[2] In this perspective, which generally ignores historical and politico-economic contexts, middle managers act along only one dimension of rationality.[3] In a technocratic, rational work setting, middle managers align their behavior with top management's goals and with larger profitability objectives; their micro-level actions in the workplace are in harmony with those macro-level purposes.

Top management charges middle managers with a dramatic mission, in this view; through their combined efforts managers must virtually ensure the life and success of the firm. March and Simon (1958), for example, argue that responsibility for motivating human beings to direct their efforts toward organizational objectives and for anticipating and managing resistance to change rests in the hands of managers who must be sensitive to the many complex organizational and human factors that emerge from employees below them and from top management above them. In the name of efficiency, managers should halt "irrational" action in the organization and replace it with formally rational actions (Fischer

---

transcend antagonistic class relations and be bound together by a mutually beneficial set of industrial rules and norms. Dahrendorf's (1959) thesis of a "postcapitalist society" pushes the postclass framework even further, arguing that authority relations characterizing the workplace will no longer be unique. Rather, production and distribution relations will be merely a subset of the authority relations common to most spheres of modern life. Such questions are further explored in and in many ways stem from a body of literature that has debated the meaning of the separation of ownership and control of corporations (Burnham 1941; Berle and Means 1968; Zeitlin 1974).

2. For descriptive accounts of managerial behavior, see Brewer and Tomlinson (1964); Horne and Lupton (1965); Mintzberg (1975); Stewart (1976); Kotter (1982); and Hales (1986).

3. See Salaman (1978) for an excellent discussion of the ahistoricism in much organization theory and of the "organizational rhetoric" that obscures how bureaucracies function as tools of power and control for specific classes of people.

and Sirianni 1984, p. 9); they should automatically maneuver toward corporate objectives. Likewise, McGregor (1960) argues that "it is natural to expect management to be committed to the economic objectives of the industrial organization" (p. 13).

By the same token, when middle managers act irrationally themselves—that is, when they do not cooperate in maximizing top management's corporate agenda—the organizational behavior perspective assumes that managers are blocked or subverted from realizing their rational, management-identified interests. Thus top managers and consultants must look for organizational solutions that will unblock logical courses of managerial action.

Organizational theorists looking at contemporary patterns of organizational decline have recently described how the current politico-economic context shapes organizational behavior. In contrast to the earlier, ahistorical studies, the recent research examines cutbacks made necessary by economic decline and stagnation (Whetton 1980), increased competition and resulting uncertainty in formerly predictable environments (Krantz 1988), and the problems of managing mature industries in crisis (Harrigan 1988). The leaders of American organizations and corporations, these researchers argue, now face the ineluctable fact that they must transform their enterprises in order to adapt to a new environment. Specifically, they must regain control over costs, decision-making processes, and cultures to prepare their firms for a new competitive era.

Furthermore, the organizational-decline literature argues that one of the biggest obstacles to corporate adaptation is inside the firm: the ranks of managers who routinely respond to demands for a cost-effective, competitive environment with dysfunctional behavior. Whether they are seen as reacting to decline with a "threat-rigidity response" (Staw, Sandelands, and Dutton 1988), minimal innovativeness and commitment to the firm (Cameron and Zammuto 1988) or as "revert[ing] to *less mature* forms of behavior that function as more primitive defenses against anxiety" (Krantz 1988, p. 267; emphasis added), middle managers in declining American organizations are depicted as massively obstructing the national attempt to regain corporate competitiveness. These managers appear to have willfully withdrawn their commitments; because they are threatened, demoralized, and depressed, they refuse to harness their expertise to the service of change and experimentation.

The current organizational paradigm, however, has an ahistoricism all its own. Although it acknowledges the importance of the changed environment, this perspective does not question top managers' claims that American corporations have been buffeted by environmental conditions beyond top managements' control; it seldom looks at how decline and restructuring may be caused by corporate policies themselves. Consequently, those who study organizational decline all too readily concur with the draconian measures corporate leaders claim must be implemented to accomplish corporate retrenchment (downsizing, layoffs, centralization, plant closures, and whittling wage packages). Moreover, these researchers conflate means and ends by suggesting that if mid-level managers fail to comply with the techniques for restructuring corporations, they must also reject the objectives of restructuring; therefore, they must be irrational about the long-term goals and viability of the organization. Observers of organizational change fail to consider whether the *means* for carrying out new agendas are truly rational in the light of the organizational exigencies middle managers face.[4]

In sum, the organizational behavior perspective tends to view conflict as personal, psychological disturbances within

4. An entire tradition in industrial sociology and the sociology of bureaucracy should have done away with this definition of rationality, subscribed to by many contemporary organization theorists. Gouldner (1954), Blau (1955), Dalton (1959), Lupton (1963), and Crozier (1964) successfully documented the alternative logics operating at different levels of organizations. Unfortunately, there is little cross-fertilization between the two fields, and there is ample speculation about why this is so (Hirsch 1975).

firms, rather than evidence of possible conflict over the boundaries of managerial autonomy or the reformulation of corporate objectives in the context of capital accumulation processes. Resistance and conflict are conceptualized as evidence of irrationality, bounded rationality, narrow self-interest, and, in some cases, products of human nature. Rarely are middle managers considered to hold interests that are consciously, rather than unintentionally, opposed to the objectives of capitalists and top management.

The second reigning orthodoxy, the "class" perspective, ironically shares the assumptions of the postclass model about the rationality of managerial action and interests. I say "ironically" because, although the question of managerial interests is analytically integral to their work, class theorists either insufficiently explain the origins and dimensions of those interests or describe them a priori (Wood 1982).

Studies of the labor process best represent the class perspective on management and control. The "coercion-and-control" model, sparked by Braverman's (1974) work, does not question but rather assumes that middle managers' interests are an extension of top management's. Middle managers rationalize and degrade the labor process of their workers without question; their objectives are thoroughly aligned with profitability objectives formulated by top management. Although Braverman suggests that managers' work, like everyone's work under monopoly capitalism, will become proletarianized in the long run, these diametrically opposed characterizations of middle management are ultimately dead ends for anyone wishing to understand the actions and interests of middle managers: managers either are capitalist agents completely in control or are hurtled into the degraded ranks of laborers, workers who are completely out of control.[5]

The "class-struggle" model, exemplified in the work of Edwards (1979), posits managers' interests and actions in a sim-

---

5. Others working in the Braverman tradition include Kraft (1977) and Zimbalist (1979).

ilarly a priori fashion. Although Edwards sees class antagonism between workers and managers as an ever-present
dynamic in the capitalist workplace, he assumes a fit between
the structures of control designed by top management and
middle managers' consent to those structures. Thus the class-
struggle model offers only partial explanations for distinctions among managers and for the way in which corporate
strategies for controlling workers transform managerial work
as well.[6]

The coercion-and-control and the class-struggle frameworks base their model of managerial action on managers as
rational representatives of capitalists and top managers. They
tend to focus almost exclusively on the ways that supervisorial and managerial personnel are agents of capital in deskilling and degrading workers. Moreover, these models tend to
lump all managers into one interest group and to make asser-
tions about management ideology without investigating how
that ideology emerges from the real conditions of managerial
work and social relations (Nichols 1980).

In these perspectives, middle managers push strategic
management's demands through without question; there is
little understanding of the divergences between middle and
strategic managers over strategies for accumulation and the
micro-level measures for achieving them. Thus both the organizational perspective and some working in the labor process perspective emphasize one basis for rational management action: the broad profit maximizing objectives of the
firm, formulated by top management, and shared and acted
on by middle managers.[7]

6. Others working in the class struggle tradition include Friedman (1977) and Clawson (1980).
7. With the exception of Wood's (1989) critical work on flexible
manufacturing, the class theorists largely have not investigated the
impact of corporate restructuring of the 1980s on the labor process.
The perspective is important, nevertheless, because of its insistence
that changes in the workplace are embedded in changes in capital-
accumulation processes. The organizational behavior theorists, in-

The "consent-and-resistance" framework, a third model, which examines how interests are shaped by particular organizational work contexts (Burawoy 1979), goes beyond these limitations. Rather than assume that there is anything preordained about workers' or managers' interests, this model emphasizes the conditions under which workers have given and withheld their consent to management objectives in the labor process under monopoly capitalism (Burawoy 1979). The study presented here begins with this emphasis and focuses on the other side of the labor relationship: the conditions under which particular managerial interests are constructed and how managers become engaged in the manufacture of consent in the workplace.

What was the managing out process and how was it related to corporate restructuring processes? Managing out was a new and distinctive practice that defined a hitherto undistinguished category of employees as poor performers. Strategic management demanded that lower-level managers, across the firm, move actively to get rid of "nonproductive" employees. Beyond those who were normally recalcitrant, uncooperative, or slow, the newly constructed definition of an unproductive employee included employees who were "deadwood" and "rigid bureaucrats with a fear of ambiguity." Managers were to "manage" and "root out" mediocrity, to "be more objective in assessing real performance," and to "make more decisions at lower levels" about firing people.

Using ranking procedures to place employees on a normal curve, managers could identify poor performers. Those who fell at the bottom of the ranked curve would be managed out as poor performers. Thus the new category of poor performer

---

cluding those who earlier studied bureaucracies, have not fully appreciated this linkage. See Clegg and Dunkerly (1980), Salaman and Thompson (1980), and Reed (1985) for a critical perspective on and possible synthesis of labor process and organization theory; see Clegg (1981) for a highly abstract class theory of intramanagement relations from an organizational perspective.

was a weapon in the war to get middle managers to use coercive management practices and to absorb responsibility for cutting the number of bank employees.

In addition, the framework of "coercive autonomy" encouraged managers to use their discretion, or managerial judgment, to subject employees to new norms intended to increase productivity. In the chapters that follow I demonstrate that in fact managers extensively used the discretion that strategic management encouraged—but not in the service of the more insidious aspects of corporate restructuring. Rather, striving to maintain and raise productivity levels to meet the larger objectives of corporate profitability, they used their discretion to fend off both the coercive application of norms and an arbitrary or purely statistical orientation toward managing out. They reinterpreted the concept of managerial discretion, focusing on organizing consent and stability and simultaneously working to increase performance levels in a context of centralization, contraction, and uncertainty.

But do middle managers really respond in such a unitary fashion? Can we substantiate claims for such undifferentiated patterns of managerial action? To answer that question we must consider the hypothesis that the uneven patterns of management restructuring shaped different organizational capacities for maneuvering against strategic management's agenda. Comparing middle managers in three production contexts—the bank branches, the systems (research and development) division, and the credit card center—shows how the structural reorganization of the firm caused different degrees of change in managerial discretion and subsequently established the limits for different courses of action. These three cases do not constitute an exhaustive list of examples of management restructuring in American Security Bank. Rather, they represent three points on a continuum, from a work site in which an extensive degree of authority and discretion was expropriated from middle managers to a work site in which managers were given greater authority to act as agents for the restructuring agenda. Specifically, I examine different ways that autonomous discretion was expropriated from middle managers and how these distinct structural conditions shaped managers' ability to act on and interpret strategic management policies.

Restructuring Branch Management

Loretta Swan had just received a monthly report on her branch the day before our interview.[8] Written by her area manager,[9] this report contained pages of statistical summaries on the "output" of her branch: checking and savings account levels, number of loan referrals, sales figures on the increasing array of financial products, and number of customer conversions to the electronic teller system and to the "checkless" checking account. Many of these transactions were aggregated by the identification number of individual tellers or customer service representatives. The report also provided detailed information on staffing and personnel, such as the number of full- and part-time positions, the number of overtime hours, and the ratios of profits to salary expenses.

The synopsis, as Loretta called it, concluded that her branch was overstaffed by one and one-half positions.[10] In the year

8. Since the changes in her job were typical of the changes in branch managers' jobs throughout the bank, Loretta Swan's case well illustrates the common patterns of change. The sample of branch managers that I interviewed included ten women and eight men. I was told by the management development division that this was roughly representative of the ratio of women to men for the larger population of branch managers, although I was unable to obtain precise figures. Interview material with branch managers was supplemented by retrospective accounts from other managers who once worked in the branch system but who, by the time of our interview, were working elsewhere in the bank.

9. Each branch was a member of an area management group (AMG); each area management group had approximately ten to fifteen branches; and each AMG had an area manager who coordinated all AMG policies.

10. The synopsis replaced the annual "time allowance sheet" (TAS) used in the past to judge average branch productivity. The TAS was, according to Neil Golden, formerly employed by the methods re-

preceding our interview she had acted on the directive of similar reports and had pared the number of full-time merchant
and customer tellers and customer service positions to fifteen
from twenty-one by not replacing employees who quit or who
moved on in the corporation, a process she called "managing
down through attrition." One of Loretta's first comments captured the meaning of the area management report to her. The
computer printout, she said, gave "unequivocal" evidence that
at that point she had to cut even more, but "everyone here
already feels overworked to death." That discouragement and
the event to which it referred aptly summarized both the
pressures on the branch manager of American Security Bank
and the hierarchical relationship between the branch and the
area management group (AMG).

The AMG was the source of much that was closing in on
the branch and contributing to a fundamental speedup of
branch operations. In many ways, the AMG was replacing the
branch, or middle management, position. It was a repository
of the management function, consolidating into one structure
a centralized mechanism for indirectly managing many smaller
bank units. The consolidation of management into the AMG
signaled the end to both the "brick and mortar" strategy of
branch growth and the decentralized structure on which that
strategy was based.

The AMG's presence was vividly embodied in the regular
summaries of branch activities that provided detailed, hard
evidence of deficiencies in productivity and overstaffing at
Loretta's branch. Loretta's own information-management
tasks, in part, enabled the AMG to amass those statistics. She
compiled information, for example, on employees' work hours,

---

search section as an operating index of staff efficiency. If a branch
failed to reach an acceptable efficiency level branch managers turned
to a time-allowance procedures manual containing guidelines for
productivity. Golden claimed that there was little pressure to control operating expenses; as long as the branch was profitable nobody
worried about branch operations. This claim would confirm the
growth/efficiency trade-off hypothesis suggested in Chapter 2.

hours employees spent in specialized training classes, and numbers of customers that tellers "converted" to products that were more profitable to the bank. But her role in gathering and summarizing information was bypassed, to some degree, by functional and technological reorganization. When tellers made loan referrals—when they arranged for a customer to obtain and submit a loan application—their names and branch were included on a referral sheet that was forwarded to and tabulated at the loan center and sent to the appropriate AMG. Information summarizing tellers' attitudes and aptitudes was gathered and quantified by anonymous shoppers, employees of the bank who routinely "shopped" at various branches and evaluated tellers' personalities (Does he or she smile? Are they pleasant?) and sales capacities (What, if any, products or services did this teller attempt to sell? Did tellers seem to have adequate knowledge of the product? Were they able to answer questions readily?).[11] The results of shopper surveys as well were forwarded to AMGs.

Even when Loretta did tabulate statistical information, the role she once played in evaluating and acting on that information had changed. Whereas formerly Loretta would have tracked branch information and used it to develop an integrated picture of branch performance, the job of tracking various kinds of information had been transferred into specialized sections in the AMG. In the branch, for example, they recorded all cash transactions over $10,000 (which they were required by law to track), but these transactions were then monitored and evaluated by one individual who followed such transactions for all branches in Loretta's area group. In this fashion, one of the functions typically ascribed to middle management—gathering and processing data on production—had been displaced by the breakdown and consolida-

11. Hochschild (1983) comments on similar attempts to reduce workers' personalities to a commodity in her study of flight attendants. Under competitive market conditions, service sector workers' ability to perform emotionally may become the object of rationalization.

tion of portions of branch management into other specialized, standardized functional locations.

The AMG issued regular directives about rationalizing the branch system. Each AMG had small teams whose purpose was to devise new ways of performing jobs and increasing branch output, techniques to be implemented in all the branches. They ranged from efforts to improve the reliability of the financial base of the bank (Loretta's AMG, for example, was working on a pilot program to screen potential accounts, allowing the bank to check customers' financial backgrounds), to rationalizing a system of flexible labor to fill in at branches on a temporary basis (a floating, on-call service staff). Some AMGs also organized quality circles in branches. But the most significant of these tasks was the rationalization of the area group as a whole. The AMG supervised branch closings and consolidations on the orders of the regional policy groups, as mandated at the divisional level.

Loretta's branch, located on a commercial strip close to residential neighborhoods, was typical of many other American Security branches. For decades this urban branch had been an integrated and semi-autonomous service center: it served local clients with personal loans and savings and checking accounts. Many of its clients grew up with the American Security branch system and developed close banking ties with branch personnel. In addition, Loretta's branch made loans to the myriad small businesses that populated the area. Driving through almost any California city one could find similar integrated American Security Bank branches, vivid testimony to American Security's widespread brick and mortar growth strategy.

The high density of bank branches and the corresponding ratio of branches to customers had changed considerably over the two years before my interview. Loretta, who had worked in the branch system for twenty years, viewed this change as extremely dramatic. She counted three branches nearby that strategic management had closed in the preceding year and a half. Bank officials estimated that nearby branches could expect to acquire approximately 3,000 new accounts as a result of a branch closing. Thus, as the number of her branch personnel was decreasing, new savings and checking accounts were shifting over to Loretta's branch.

To address this problem in part, an electronic teller had been installed outside the front door.[12] Theoretically many bank transactions would be transferred from the tellers inside the branch to the electronic teller outside.[13] Indeed, one of the productivity goals in the AMG report was to increase electronic teller usage by 60 percent. Tellers were supposed to work at "converting" clients to the electronic teller; but then, they were also supposed to "sell" financial products across the counter and rarely had time to devote to either task. The "conversion rate" quota in the AMG report fell on Loretta's shoulders; as branch manager she was cast in the role of selling and legitimating the new technology to the bank's customers, convincing long-term clients, who had had personalized banking relations for years and were prejudiced against the new machinery, to begin using the depersonalized, often intimidating withdrawal and deposit technology.

Responsibility for rationalizing other functional and organizational changes to customers also fell on Loretta's shoulders. Bank clients regularly sought her out to complain when branches with which they had done business for years suddenly closed. Customers from neighboring areas were now forced not only to trek over to her branch but also to use electronic transaction procedures.

12. According to an early analysis of the benefits of the electronic teller system, the system enabled the bank to avoid replacing 3,000 employees in the branch system who left their jobs; the system also facilitated branch closure, allowing replacement of a branch by one or two electronic tellers.

13. The electronic teller system was one of a number of automated mechanisms used to bypass the branch structure of banking. One system allowed customers to bank from their homes on personal computers, while on-site electronic payments systems bypassed the branch network by eliminating the need for check or cash transactions.

Perhaps the biggest functional change was the disappearance of the accessible and personalized lending apparatus. Branch top management centralized lending into specialized divisions, reflecting the bank's commitment to targeting and profiting from stratified market segments. As a result, all loan activities were routed around the branch system itself. The differentiation of the lending function into specialized units removed a significant source of Loretta's authority. She no longer had authority to make loans, nor did she manage loan personnel, a capacity that historically had qualified her for a higher job grade than the branch administrative officer (the branch manager's assistant).

By 1985 all lending officers had been removed from this branch; now, if anyone submitted a loan application, Loretta forwarded it to the appropriate consumer, real estate, or commercial loan center. She personally had loan quotas to fill, but, like tellers, her role in selling loans was strictly one of referral. And if the loan did not go through she did not receive credit for it. Loretta remarked that "branch managers are supposed to give the appearance of being salespersons; but their presence is largely symbolic." The cheery banner that stretched across her branch, exhorting "Need a loan? Call 800-
. . ." did little to obscure the stark fact that the majority of individuals or small businesses had to pursue loans through impersonal, centralized sources. The red phone perched in the branch lobby, providing a direct hot line to the loan center, only accentuated the distance and anonymity of the new lending process.

Another important aspect of branch managers' work was siphoned off in this period, as strategic management ordered the centralization of personnel management into the AMG. At one time Loretta would have approved or disapproved a simple performance plan and taken appropriate action on awarding pay raises (within her branch budget). In a system of area management, branch managers no longer possessed ultimate authority to evaluate and approve an employee's performance. Loretta would forward the performance evaluation plans, which had been written by her assistant (the branch administrative officer) and approved by Loretta, to her own manager at the AMG. The new PPCE and the extensive documentation it contained provided the area manager with the information required for indirect management: in other words, it gave area managers more control over individual branches. The PPCE linked the AMG to branch employees in an apparatus of accountability; it could be used as a basis of decision making about rewarding employees or managing them out. For Loretta, the new system severed an important link between evaluating and directing those she managed, on the one hand, and rewarding them, on the other.

A new link, however, was put in place in 1984. Employees seeking other jobs within the corporation were no longer able to apply for those jobs entirely on their own: the internal labor market was not an open one. As part of the new "career management" program, branch employees were required to solicit Loretta's written permission when they applied for other bank jobs, in effect confirming that the employee was available and qualified to apply. Thus Loretta was still an important link in the path of mobility.

Group area managers scrutinized the PPCEs, and they reranked all branch employees by merging them into a pool of all employees in the area group. Loretta was also ranked against managers from the other branches in her area. For her own evaluation, she met with her AMG manager and a human resources committee. She was, she said, ranked as part of a separate middle management curve; as a result of her last evaluation session, two managers in her area who had received fairly low rankings left their branch management jobs and entered jobs with lower grades.[14] Loretta also lost her flexible, branch-level hiring privileges. The AMG determined the parameters of hiring: if Loretta were given permission to hire in her branch, it would be someone from the pool of the redeployed.

Loretta thus had an intermediary role grounded in the lin-

14. Loretta was previously evaluated by management at the regional level, but she was not ranked against a normal curve.

gering symbolic authority of the branch manager. She was to improve the work performance of branch employees, but in fact the AMG was the final arbiter of wages and promotions. The position was an uneasy one, for Loretta felt she had few grounds on which to justify why branch employees did not receive salary increases and why, when no replacements for those who had left were in sight, she was unable to gain approval for a "rec" (a requisition for new branch employees). Still, the PPCE did have to pass through Loretta's hands before going to the area manager for approval; this small act, plus the fact that she still was top management's representative in the branch, made Loretta feel that she still had some degree of leverage with her employees.

In a very bald way, her AMG manager looked to her to manage and legitimate the disruptive aspects of the major corporate changes that were taking place. On the one hand, she would receive summary reports stating that her branch was overstaffed, even when the number of employees had declined through attrition. Yet while the AMG mandated lower staffing levels, it simultaneously called on Loretta to cover up the bank's larger goal of cutting personnel. The tension between these two roles—cutting staff and covering up staff reductions—emerged explicitly when she (and all branch managers) received a "communiqué" ordering her to hold staff meetings to tell employees that the bank had no intention of engaging in layoffs. Thus the AMG required branch managers both to implement staff cuts based on statistical criteria and to reassure bank employees that systematic staff cuts were not taking place.

The growing similarity between managers' work and tellers' work exacerbated the uneasiness of the manager's role. Loretta spent a significant amount of time "on the line": working in the capacity of teller, she enabled her declining staff to meet branch business. From the perspective of branch business as a whole, Loretta's work as a teller filled critical gaps in branch staffing. In other words, the speedup of branch operations was predicated on the "demanagerialization" of Loretta's position.

New sales quotas on her own PPCE meant that the teller window was an advantageous location from which she could approach customers about purchasing an IRA, a safety deposit box, or one of the many types of checking accounts. But as Loretta crossed the occupational boundary line into the ranks of teller, and faced "production quotas" very similar to those of her tellers and customer service representatives, she felt increasingly ineffective as a representative of the decisions of the AMG.

Certain ingredients of branch managers' jobs were transferred to and consolidated in the AMG. Another displacement of the management function consisted of upgrading lower-level employees and authorizing them to take over other tasks. A balance of power between Loretta and her tellers shifted in relation to changes in her position as an ultimate source of approval for certain shop-floor transactions. The bank had upgraded some tellers to the status of corporate officer, which entailed special training and lowering the cutoff point of officer status to encompass the job grade that included tellers. As officers, tellers were vested with authority to approve transactions hitherto confined to higher levels of supervision. Thus, for example, tellers were gaining the authority to authorize transaction amounts and types of checks for which they previously had needed the authorization of either a supervisor (branch administrative officer) or branch manager. Upgrading transactional authority by upgrading tellers paved the way for eliminating on-site management of daily operations.

Branch Managers and Managing Change

Many of the changes in the branch system were enduring and absolute. As personnel and operations management were transferred into the area management group, branch managers were managed and monitored more actively than ever before. Although this restructuring process may have sharply circumscribed their room for maneuver, branch managers did act on the restructuring processes that were so radically transforming their workplace. Organizational restructuring could not strip branch managers of their capacity to organize work processes within the branch or to use their accumulated expertise to find different ways to increase branch productivity. Nor could it completely eliminate managers' interests in engendering consent to increased productivity. Branch managers received orders from above, yet reinterpreted them, linking the new agenda with their own production constraints.

Branch managers were pressured to do more with fewer employees. Faced as they were with demands to increase productivity (by AMG reports and by the objectives written into managers' PPCEs to reduce staff), branch managers were to manage out employees who were at the bottom of the ranked curve in their branches. Managing out, according to Loretta, would further strain a situation in which current staff were already exceedingly stretched. She needed to maintain a certain staff level to meet branch business, even if some tellers were not as fast as others and some lacked total comprehension of all the new bank products (which numbered well over a hundred).

Moreover, she felt that if the burden of restructuring were individualized in this way, she would have great difficulty maintaining her "managerial legitimacy," however tenuous. The slow and arduous mechanics of managing out would, she claimed, have an extremely demoralizing impact on remaining staff and resources. She would have to identify and start coaching her lowest performers, cautioning them that if they did not meet new productivity levels they might be put on probation; she had to seek approval from her manager and consult with various personnel specialists and occasionally lawyers to determine whether she or the bank might be liable for a discrimination suit.

Branch managers followed an alternative path to the individualizing strategy of managing out employees. They instead turned their efforts toward increasing the productivity of their branch as a whole by managing up their employees.

Often organizing team or group efforts, sometimes utilizing a language of self-management, branch managers focused on managing up the performance of the unit by mobilizing their employees, individually and in groups, to work harder. This unit-centered strategy allowed managers both to avoid intense privatization and individualization of their daily managerial relations and to comply with the larger objective of recapturing the bank's competitive edge.

Managers employed a number of measures to improve the productivity of their branches: they worked on line with the tellers; managed up individual employees by pushing them to sell more products and to convert more customers to new deposit, withdrawal, and checking procedures and by pushing them to attend more and diverse training classes; organized branch employees into quality circles (which were, without exception, geared to finding productivity improvements for the branch); and obtained greater employee participation in establishing and working toward new and higher personal objectives on the performance planning forms. As long as performance plans still passed through the hands of the branch manager, he or she continued to use the PPCE to set higher objective levels for employees. Branch managers' efforts thus were localized within the branch as they attempted to organize and elicit greater cooperation from their employees to respond to new pressures.

Working to increase the productivity of the branch as a whole was one defense against having systematically to apply arbitrary criteria for managing out individuals, a process both personally painful and organizationally costly. In this way, branch managers used the few sources of organizational leverage remaining to them to influence the direction of the corporate restructuring process; they avoided politicizing their daily managerial relations and tried to focus employees' efforts on improving the performance of the branch. Through the unit-centered strategy, however, they also attempted to fend off the "final directive" from the AMG: the order to close the branch.

Loretta, for example, explicitly saw herself as fending off the demise of her own branch. To this end she strove to overcome her tellers' resistance to "selling" customers on the electronic teller system (they disliked having to do this because customers themselves resisted abandoning their personalized relations with human tellers). She also pushed tellers to attend and participate in product training and documentation classes so that her branch would remain competitive with other branches (employee training and productivity were compared with other branch employees in the AMG). Besides coaching individuals about the need for training, she organized tellers to meet before the branch opened for brief informational sessions about the work ahead of them and to travel as a group to attend classes.

She did these things despite the tellers' angry claims that they were "never left alone" and were constantly being pushed to train in new areas. Persuading employees to meet and exceed new quotas was a more credible approach to the strained situation in her branch than trying to edge already scarce workers out of the branch office. Although branch managers had little power over decision making about branch closures, her efforts were devoted to managing up the productivity of her workers to ensure the survival of the branch.

In a somewhat atypical, but nevertheless illustrative, approach to branch problems, a few branch managers sought collective reinforcement for their attempts to increase branch productivity at the group level. After attending a management training seminar, dissatisfied with the individualizing effects of the new policies and pressures, and with the isolation they felt under the slew of directives emanating from their AMG, Meredith King and a fellow branch manager organized a one-day seminar for their assistant managers and a few of their top employees. They rented a hotel room, ordered takeout food, and spent one Saturday systematically going over some of the new "rules and regulations" to develop, as they put it, a common framework from which they could all face the many pressures facing them in their work. Hypothetical conflict situations between managers and nonmanagerial employees were "role played"; new branch quotas, the mechanics of PPCEs, salary packages, and the crisis conditions facing the bank were discussed.

Meredith's seminar was symbolically and organizationally important. Forming lateral ties with a manager in a similar position legitimized her efforts and helped her gain the confidence of her employees. By conducting the seminar on her own time and at her own and her fellow manager's expense, Meredith relayed the message that she was pooling her efforts with those of her workers, rather than simply expecting them to bear the full brunt of increasing productivity. In other words, this outside seminar provided an additional opportunity for persuasion and manipulation. She appealed to her employees' loyalties and commitments in a highly personalized setting; she used the language and process of the team approach to let them know how much she depended on them and to gain their compliance to the new productivity goals of the branch.

To accentuate the importance of their heightened participation, Meredith also emphasized the possible negative outcomes corporate restructuring could have on her employees' jobs. This tactic was shared by another branch manager, Norma Levinworth. Norma rejected the notion that a good manager was opaque and that she should privatize the impact of the restructuring process. Striving for a process that would produce results similar to the ones Meredith King achieved in her day-long seminar, Norma held regular meetings with her branch employees to keep them informed of what she knew about ongoing branch closures, and what she had heard, if anything, about their branch. She used these meetings also to point out problems that might arise as a result of staff reduction through redeployment and pressures on tellers to sell new products with less time to do so. Employees as a group strategized ways to confront these pressures.

These examples point out how branch managers worked around the demand, promoted in the seminar, that they should

obfuscate top management's agenda and the facts about corporate restructuring. They instead used a method of transparent management for their own purposes. Loretta rejected that
demand in another way: when she met with her employees to
assure them that there would be no layoffs (following the orders of her communiqué) she refused to understate the situation. She prepared a presentation detailing the economics of
the branch and the continued pressures that employees should
expect, despite the absence of formal layoffs.

Thus, even though she could reassure her branch workers
to some degree, she called for a collective response by publi-
cizing selected facts about the crisis situation. In the eyes of
strategic management, Meredith, Norma, and Loretta committed the sin of being transparent managers. But they calculated that hiding the truth about corporate restructuring
could be more costly, with respect to maintaining a stable
level of operations and the trust of their employees, than exposing employees to the crisis of the bank. Their response was
to depict the pressures on the branch as something that could
be met only by collective, group efforts.

The strategy of deliberate transparency coincided with another pattern in which branch managers promoted greater
group effort by advocating self-management of the workplace. To some degree it would be correct to see middle managers' interests in self-management as evidence of self-coer-
cion: by pushing responsibility downward, branch managers
were ostensibly organizing themselves out of functional positions. One might even hypothesize that where managers' jobs
were threatened, they might react in quite a different way.
They might espouse anti-self-management philosophies or try
to protect their managerial status even more by embracing
some philosophy of the importance of hierarchy and the role
of managers in maintaining it.

Indeed, at times branch managers' articulation of the issue
of self-management seemed to run directly counter to their
own positional interests. Brian Corning adamantly assured
me that he was "not a manager, not a supervisor, but a facil-

itator. People should take responsibilities; employees have to take more risks." In this role he tried to get branch workers to sell financial services more actively, to generate ideas collectively for coping efficiently with longer lines of customers, and to strategize ways that workers could take more responsibility for branch affairs. Brian's statement, and the statements of others who advocated decentralized responsibility in these terms, seemed to suggest that branch managers were simply and blindly managing themselves out of jobs. But in fact, the middle-managerial ideology of self-management and decentralization intersected with a struggle for the very existence of their jobs and of the branch itself.

Managers facilitated the demanagerialization of their workplace, espousing self-management in an ongoing attempt to improve the performance of the branch and stave off possible branch closure. Because the ultimate criteria for closing branches were factors outside branch managers' control, they tried to find daily work mechanisms through which they, as managers with an integral role in facilitating productivity, could enhance a group effort and thus branch profitability to the greatest degree possible.

Self-management did not entail the elimination of managers' jobs, in their view; greater initiative, and therefore productivity, on the shop floor was made possible through the efforts of managers.[15] By encouraging branch employees to take more responsibility for branch productivity and to be more attuned to the general crisis of the bank, branch managers believed they had a better chance of avoiding branch closure in the long run.[16]

15. Clearly, branch managers' concept of self-management differs dramatically from the view of self-management in which workers would have the means to direct the affairs of the workplace autonomously (cf. Blumberg 1975). Conventional definitions notwithstanding, these managers used the term to describe a change in the division of labor and the participative group effort they were promoting.

16. This corresponds to Nichols and Beynon's (1977) observation, in a study of the transformation of management in a British chemi-

This link between ideology and branch survival shed light on another paradox: how branch managers discussed concepts such as entrepreneurialism and risk taking. On first encountering these concepts in our interviews, I was struck by the incompatibility between genuine entrepreneurialism and work life in a large corporation that was visibly contracting. However, these ideologies became less paradoxical when branch managers explained them in terms of efforts devoted to branch survival. As they elaborated their precise definitions of entrepreneurialism or risk taking under the conditions they faced, they referred to working harder, getting their hands "dirty" on the line, and engaging in nonmanagerial work tasks.

Evidence of business overload in Adele Silverstein's branch was vivid. In the stately lobby of her enormous metropolitan branch, the velvet ropes that channeled lines of people as they waited for a teller had recently been restrung to accommodate increasing numbers of customers. The new lines wove back and forth five or six times, nearly filling the large lobby. This branch no longer had a manager; Adele, as the branch administrative officer, reported directly to her area manager (her AMG happened to be located in the upper floors of this immense building).

Adele Silverstein assured me that she had always been a risk taker. This meant to her that she was never hidden away in her branch office, directing the branch from afar; she "risked" herself by stepping down into the nonmanagement ranks, working side by side with nonmanagerial employees. Her definition of risk taking also was colored throughout by a philosophy of decentralized responsibility and greater worker participation. In the context of the bank's financial crisis, she felt that more than ever managers must step down from the managerial pedestal and encourage bank employees to start

---

cal company, that managers may put their technical knowledge at the disposal of workers when everyone is threatened by unemployment (p. 72).

"turning a profit for themselves [taking greater responsibility for overall branch business] by being more profitable for the company." Her worry that managers might "hide behind their management status," that they might not plunge into the gritty work of daily business, had a very practical component. Strategic management was targeting managers under the current branch reconfiguration plan, and even branch administrative officers like herself might gradually be phased out. Adele felt that taking risks and having the courage to abandon the managerial role occasionally might ultimately contribute to branch survival.

It is significant, then, that branch managers did not reject the notion of entrepreneurialism out of hand. In contrast to the organizational-behavior researchers' claims that middle managers refuse to innovate or to embrace the idea of working in entrepreneurial ways, these branch managers were extremely innovative, although they used different criteria from those spelled out for them by the bank's top managers. Their definition of entrepreneurialism was infused with a content that corresponded to their practical situations.

Finally, in the context of centralization, demands for greater productivity and managers' aversion to proceeding with the managing-out process, branch managers' attitudes toward layoffs instigated by top management become comprehensible. Loretta's and others' statements that layoffs were a critical remedy to their managing situation at first seemed perplexing; their personnel shortages and concomitant demands for greater productivity suggested that the least desirable policy in the world would be further staff reductions. Considering the available options, however, Loretta felt that top-management-initiated layoffs would provide a legitimacy that she could not personally provide in her role as a "cheerleader" for corporate reorganization—a term that she used bitterly, referring to being compelled to represent top management in managing an enormous amount of stress in her branch.

Her endorsement of more systematic layoffs reflected her

feelings of powerlessness to create the kind of workplace in which she knew top management was ultimately interested: a dramatically pared down branch system staffed with workers who unquestioningly went along with work speed-ups and job cuts. Managers' unit-centered strategies, which focused on managing up, and their refusal to manage out thus were reinforced by their global critique of strategic management's mishandling of the bank restructuring.

Dan Wong, another long-term branch manager, shared Loretta's criticisms. The story that American Security Bank was not laying off its employees was "almost a myth," he succinctly claimed, and the underlying reality of what managers were being asked to do placed insurmountable pressures on them.

> Top management should just as well come out and say exactly what's going on. People resent when they're told they're lucky to have a job [he had said that managers were supposed to employ this argument as ammunition for the managing-out process] or that if they can't accept change, then they're out. The practice of policies in the bank don't match the rhetoric of the top administration.

The tension managers experienced when trying to manage out had driven several of Dan's friends in other branch management positions to resign flat out from their jobs.[17]

The fact that many managers were moving into AMGs or transitional occupations may have served to confine these strategies to in-branch relations: such lateral mobility could

17. IBM's workers and managers have had similar responses to the firm's "invisible layoffs" (*Wall Street Journal*, 8 April 1987). Several groups of dissident workers (assemblers, technicians, and salespeople) attempted to organize unions as a response to what they saw as top management's attempts to cut the work force by firings and forced transfers (*Wall Street Journal*, 13 January 1987). These workers claimed that IBM to all intents and purposes abandoned its no-layoff policy while professing otherwise. For a very different interpretation of IBM's redeployment program which stresses openness of communication, cooperation, and maximization of the interests of all involved, see Greenhalgh, McKersie, and Gilkey (1986).

disguise the demise of branch management.[18] Branch managers occasionally moved into specialized positions within the AMG (some managerial, some not; often a manager would become part of the team that developed productivity innovations for the branch system or work as an assistant to an area manager, coordinating specialized groups and acting as an informational liaison with remaining branch managers).[19] Or they might step into a position created by the restructuring of the bank (one woman, after working as a branch manager for over fifteen years, became a relocations counselor; she provided advice in such areas as housing, schooling, and moving to SystemsGroup employees and their families who were transferring to a new location forty miles away). Other managers were shuffled around, "redeployed," on short notice, to fill in at another branch (to work temporarily as a branch administrative officer, for example) or called in to oversee the conversion of a full-service branch to a limited-service convenience banking center.

This diffusion of their energies, however, did not altogether eradicate branch managers' larger criticism of pressures wrought on them by the new corporate agenda. Ron Corleone's branch was a mirror image of Loretta Swan's. Lo-

18. One branch manager, however, told me of several branch managers who had grouped together formally to protest the closing of a branch in their immediate area, a busy urban district. They felt that the closing would have a detrimental impact on the work load of the surrounding branches. The group appeared to have had little impact; the branch was closed, and this informant was unsure whether the group had pursued any strategies against the reconfiguration of the branch system. This was the one example in which branch managers took their grievances outside the branch to upper levels of management.

19. One of the paradoxes of the AMG—particularly insofar as the AMG was actively involved in rationalizing and reducing the scope of the branch system—was that this unit was staffed by displaced branch managers from closed and shrinking branches. Their new work was explicitly directed at reconfiguring the organization of branch management. In other words they applied their expertise about branch operations to further expropriate the organizational bases for autonomous branch middle management.

cated on the other side of the city, it was in an area with a similar mixture of residential and business units; it also serviced long-term customers. From his perspective, having worked in the branch system for twenty-eight years, Ron felt less and less like a manager as he spent more time on the branch floor compensating for the lack of resources (staff) to meet the needs of a branch made vastly busier by surrounding branch closures.

He was very angry about the pressures to which the contracting conditions were subjecting his branch; he saw them as directly related to strategic management's past inattention to long-run financial health: "Top management should have started modernizing years ago—other banks were doing it and now we are in a real mess." He felt that these pressures demoralized the employees on whom he increasingly depended to achieve branch objectives. Ron spoke fearfully of cases he knew in which branch managers like himself were displaced by branch administrative officers who had a lower grade classification and were thus paid less for branch management duties. With the AMG actually managing personnel evaluation and reward, staffing levels, and productivity from afar, management within the branch was increasingly restricted to supervising and daily on-line operational procedures.

The overhaul of corporate culture served only to stoke other branch managers' criticism of strategic management. On returning from the management training seminar, the supervisors Adele Silverstein managed were very angry about the discrepancy between what they were "taught" by seminar trainers and the realities of their workplace. Adele said that it was a big mistake for top management to introduce the principles of what she called "ideal management"—a theory of management in which managers supposedly have time to work intensely with individual employees—when in fact managers were always responsible for too many people.[20] Their

20. The difficulties of having to manage ever greater numbers of employees partially explains why branch managers adopted group

responsibilities had expanded so much that the new demand to spend 30 percent of their work time explicitly managing provoked a great deal of derision and cynicism.

A Branch Without Management?

The restructured bank branch reflected strategic management's commitment to reducing the branch to a bare-bones operation. As strategic management systematically scaled down the branch system (reducing both numbers of employees and the size of the infrastructure); separated the bulk of retail banking ("mass" banking) from smaller, potentially more profitable private banking groups; differentiated the lending function out into centralized centers subject to greater control; capitalized on new electronic technologies that enabled customers to bypass the traditional organization of the branch; and cut levels of management, it was clear that the branch of old would no longer be American Security's primary and profitable unit of production. The new branch structure would instead serve the less profitable mass market in the most scaled-down, rationalized fashion possible.

A key to rationalizing branch operations was doing away with the decentralized management structure, a major source of branch autonomy. But if this were to happen, what organizational structure would supersede this managerial arrangement?

Loretta spoke with some fear of the possibility that her branch would suffer the same fate as that of a nearby branch and be turned into a "superbranch." Twenty-four employees at that branch had been put on "staff-available" status (when an employee was redeployed they entered a pool of people available for other staff positions in the bank). As part of a pilot program they were replaced by twelve handpicked "supertellers" who were given the status of corporate officers.

----

strategies over the individual strategy of managing out. The latter was extremely time-consuming.

Those tellers had very high transaction limits, opened new accounts, and in general worked with mass market customers—those with relatively unspecialized transactional needs. Their sales goals, or quotas, were passed down from the AMG. The superbranch did not have a management level, but was managed by an AMG and staffed by electronic tellers and upgraded workers endowed with the authority necessary for daily operations decisions.[21]

Rather than representing the epitome of a new decentralized self-managing services delivery center, the superbranch was predicated on extremely centralized forms of control. The electronic teller system tied branch cash transactions to the centralized and computerized banking system; and the consolidated area management structure (with managers managing a number of these streamlined branches), anonymous shoppers, and the use of upgraded tellers (corporate officers) facilitated off-site management. This production organization is a form of centralized bureaucracy in which front-line workers (tellers) are given more decision-making powers.

The superbranch was not the predominant organizational form during the period of my research. More common was the convenience banking center, which was similarly scaled down but contained a few more specialized branch operations than the superbranch and had one level of management. But strategic management was clearly committed to creating a branch system that approximated the superbranch model.

The comments of Michael Flynn, manager of an AMG and

21. Other banks have picked up the model of a superbranch-like organization as well. One major California competitor recently revamped its branch system, replacing employees in twenty-six different job categories with "personal bankers" who perform a small handful of tasks interchangeably. This rationalization of jobs went hand in hand with a slowdown in branch expansion, widening of the automated teller network, centralization of the lending function, and the elimination of over 2,000 jobs. Trends in the banking industry as a whole stand as a telling backdrop to the rationalization of the branch system: one consultant suggests that the banking industry will consolidate to 40 percent of its present size by 1990, affecting nearly one million people (Wishard 1985).

former executive assistant to a top-ranking bank leader, captured strategic management's perspective on the branch in the changed banking climate of the 1980s. Reflecting on the relationship of his AMG to the current branch structure, Flynn focused on the economies of product and market differentiation contained in the new banking hierarchy. The AMG structure of management corresponded to the "real" business needs of the community—it was more flexible, in his opinion, and avoided the unproductive duplication of services and managers that the old branch system entailed. (His calculation of what communities "really" needed was based on the belief that the savings from scaling back the branch system would be passed down to customers—a questionable conclusion in view of the fact that for the first time ever the bank was charging customers for such basic services as deposit, withdrawal, and checking transactions. Furthermore, his calculations did not include the loss to many customers of personalized banking services.) He argued that the branch was no longer the appropriate unit of service; consolidating management and lending in specialized units represented a more reasonable distribution of labor and other resources.

The structural changes documented in this chapter did not, and could not, eliminate branch managers' expertise and autonomous judgment about how to manage in the context of contraction and centralization. Although centralized personnel officers specified how managers should use their judgment to cut back the organization, branch managers would actually have to negotiate the cutbacks in their work sites. It was branch managers, women and men alike, who judged that the policies of restructuring, proposed by strategic management, would have to be muted and reinterpreted so as to avoid obstructing the future prosperity of their work sites.

Strategic management's policies were intended as a quick fix for the bank's downsizing dilemma, but branch managers had to work to minimize the coercive tactics that could well undermine the consent necessary to maintain and increase productivity in the long run. Although they avoided coercion, they did not refrain from co-optation. Even if branch managers would not use punitive criteria to manage employees, they worked to avert employee resistance to job speedups and uncertainty—collective resistance on employees', not managers', terms; individual and group resistance in the form of extreme demoralization and possible slowdowns or sabotage.

It was managers who put their technical knowledge to the service of workers, applying their expertise to the organization of work to ensure adaptation to structural and economic transformations. In this way branch managers managed on an alternative definition of the corporate interest, a definition that explicitly criticized strategic management's policies while endorsing corporate survival.

5

SystemsGroup:
The Leading Edge

Whereas the branch system was the object of radical down-grading processes, SystemsGroup was the source of many of those changes. When it was first organized in 1984, SystemsGroup was hailed not only as a state-of-the-art division because of its technology and its skilled employees but also as the division that would help American Security Bank gain a competitive edge in a new banking climate. SystemsGroup, a high-technology division comprising over 3,000 engineers, programmers, systems analysts, and staff, was systematically to unleash its scientific expertise onto numerous functions throughout the bank and find ways of automating or eliminating them. Its research groups developed information-management systems across the bank (linking and centralizing them through common data bases and technologies), designed systems for capturing and continually updating electronic data, and explored ways to gain greater control over bank information.

SystemsGroup was not only a cause of centralization, however; from its inception, this division was organized on a model of centralized bureaucracy. Before SystemsGroup, programmers and systems analysts were affiliated with functionally specific divisions spread over fifteen locations. In 1983, American Security hired an outsider as the bank's "technology czar," to consolidate the technology and information-management functions. In a five-year plan that cost the bank nearly $5 billion—over 40 percent of which was personnel expenses—the new czar brought SystemsGroup employees together into a sleek postmodern complex of buildings, creating a division that would "manage the application of technology as a strategic resource and as an integral part of American Security Bank's many businesses" (management literature).

The new centralized organization afforded greater control over the employment conditions and total wage package of SystemsGroup. The process of physical and organizational centralization forced SystemsGroup middle managers into a closer working relationship with the human resources staff who were to assist the bank in gaining control over wage costs. In early 1983 the president of corporate human resources announced a new organizational arrangement of the corporate personnel division. The human resources staff formerly had been concentrated in bank headquarters. That centralized personnel group was broken up, its members sent to each of the bank's nine major divisions (the retail, or branch, division, international banking, SystemsGroup, and so forth).

Although strategic management touted this change as decentralizing the human resources function and bringing "day-to-day personnel decision making closer to the divisional level," the implantation of smaller human resources groups within the major divisions was actually a more organizationally effective version of centralized personnel management. "Diffusion-centralization" more accurately describes this organizational arrangement, since it extended control by locating centralized power closer to the line.[1] Through organizational innovation, the executive-level personnel division gained direct access to its operatives at operation levels.

1. This combined decentralization and centralization paralleled the emergence of the area-management-group (AMG) organization of management, establishing a stricter path of accountability between the regional groups and the branch system.

Thus strategic management used the human resources group to gain control over management's discretion in matters pertaining to employment conditions and the total wage bill of SystemsGroup. Much like branch managers before the bank reorganized, systems managers before the formation of SystemsGroup had almost complete autonomy in hiring, initiating new projects, and approving "out-of-guideline" raises and promotions.

That autonomy was the direct object of restructuring in the newly centralized SystemsGroup division. The human resources people, physically located within the division, rationalized and standardized procedures by which SystemsGroup managers would hire, fire, and reward. They gained a new position of authority in the management circuit by creating centralized data bases for recruiting and hiring, redeploying systems workers on completion of projects, and requiring that middle managers consult with senior human resources representatives about wage packages for new employees and raises and promotions for others.

Strategic management, in mapping out SystemsGroup operations, laid the organizational bases for centralizing its key features. But the organizational future of SystemsGroup differed from that of the branch system in two important respects. First, unlike the downgrading of branch operations and employees, the "production" processes of SystemsGroup's programmers and analysts were not directly subject to rationalization (in the dynamic sense suggested by writers such as Kraft [1977] and Greenbaum [1979]), and SystemsGroup's projects were expanding rather than contracting.[2]

2. Greenbaum points out that there are efficiency trade-offs within firms between its different units. While some units are explicitly "profit centers," others provide services for bolstering efficiency in profit centers. SystemsGroup served this latter function. Different efficiency objectives may rule different departments. From the perspective of top management, the efficiency of the whole firm need not be equal to the efficiency of all its parts (Greenbaum 1979, chap. 3).

Second, strategic management was not intent on systematically displacing middle-level management in SystemsGroup, as they were middle management in the branches. SystemsGroup faced a unique future. The management process itself was an object of rationalization and centralization. The concerted effort to control yet retain managers in SystemsGroup reflects a configuration of production, labor market, and skill factors that differs significantly from that of the branch system.

The Project Group

The typical production unit in SystemsGroup, the *project group*, shaped the role of middle managers in this extremely male-dominated "high-tech" division.[3] The expertise of the project group, its collaboration as a team, and the labor market position of its members explain project-group autonomy and the subsequent demands placed on middle managers. These factors also cast light on managers' oppositions to arbitrarily defined management techniques.

Each project group consisted of a project manager (first-line management) and four to ten programmers and systems analysts (associate systems engineers, systems engineers, advisory systems engineers, and senior consultants) who analyzed user needs, conceptualized how those information or technological needs could be met, and executed the project collectively.

These projects operated in cycles with lives of three months to three years. A group developed new products and services and maintained or modified them. Projects were undertaken at the request of users throughout the bank; requests num-

3. In SystemsGroup, I interviewed five group managers, all men; two women project managers; four human resource staff members, two men and two women; and three male programmers. (The vast majority of programmers and systems analysts were men.) I also attended a meeting for human resources staff working in SystemsGroup.

bered in the hundreds each year. First-level or project managers were both co-workers and supervisors, conferring with systems people about the distribution of the various pieces of the entire project. They loosely supervised the group's activities in close conjunction with group members themselves, performed technical work on the project, and evaluated each group member, writing their performance plans and recommending promotions and raises.

Group systems managers (second-level or middle managers) managed from two to six of these group projects, directly supervising each group's project manager. The cyclical and variable aspects of project life meant that middle managers managed several projects at different stages of a cycle: as one project ended another could be in its beginning or middle stage. Middle managers acted as a liaison between the project group (the vendor) and the future product user. These managers also had to approve project managers' recommendations on raises, promotions, and firings before the recommendations were sent to human resources and divisional-level management for final authorization.

The project group exercised a good deal of control over their own pace and product. Through group consultation, and with one member acting as group leader to work closely with first-level managers—usually a senior programming consultant (Kraft calls this group hierarchy the "Chief Programmer Team" [1977, pp. 59–60])—the group designed the pieces of the project, determined appropriate staffing needs, and adjusted the distribution of the work project among themselves.

For these reasons project and group systems managers regularly reported that their role in setting quotas for those they managed was minimal. As Frank Cosgrove, a group systems manager, commented, the groups he managed consisted of "professionals who don't really need to be stretched," because they collectively designed the project, building into it individual objectives. Its collective nature was really a check on each and every member involved. Rhonda, a project manager, pointed out that her project members collectively generated and agreed on the objectives that would be written into their PPCEs. As first-line manager her job was to coordinate the project, working on it directly and coordinating its output with that of the other groups reporting to her group systems manager.

That autonomy also gave project groups room to reject demands for work intensification and speed-up. Rhonda was understaffed by two people, one employee on leave and one recently promoted. Rhonda and her manager had had difficulty hiring the additional NOMAD programmers she needed for her group.[4] With a new manager several levels above her pressuring her unit, not only for more reports, but for reports that stratified statistical information in new and more complex ways (with different time and function parameters), Rhonda's manager had to negotiate between the four project managers he managed and management above him. Using information she generated about her own group's current project and skills, Rhonda assigned priorities to work at hand, with the assistance of the project's group leader, and gave her manager a list of what they could and could not finish. He then had to negotiate upward with divisional-level management about not increasing the production of reports.

The autonomy of these nonmanagerial systems analysts and programmers was further enhanced by their comparatively strong labor market positions. Middle-level managers continually acknowledged the constraints they felt when dealing with systems employees. The fact that engineers, programmers, and systems analysts had many alternatives to employment at American Security Bank gave them another degree of leverage against centralization and rationalization. Perhaps these were the features of SystemsGroup employees—the relative autonomy, the critical role of their projects, and their advantaged labor market position—that provoked Jeremy Downs, the manager of staffing within the human resources function, to comment, " 'Manager' is a misleading term. People think

4. NOMAD is a programming language.

that managers control employees. Employees really control managers and employees can wreak havoc on a department through sabotage."

The team-project basis of production, the specialized expertise of programmers and systems people, and their labor market position all explain a high degree of autonomy and leverage on the line in SystemsGroup.[5] Kraft (1977, chap. 4) and Greenbaum (1979, pp. 116–127) confirm this analysis of group autonomy and the consequent dependence of management on group expertise. Whalley argues that this autonomy creates a fundamental tension between technical staff and capital-accumulation processes. Technical professionals "possess knowledge critical to technological development," but at the same time this knowledge "has to be harnessed to profitable production" (Whalley 1986, p. 223). Dependence on technical workers' knowledge poses an ongoing uncertainty in employers' control over the labor process. The expanding organizational environment, a result of strategic management's commitment to developing the bank's technological competitiveness, also explains a lack of pressure to rationalize work processes.[6]

Although SystemsGroup fared well compared with the branch system in the overall division of labor of the bank, it was not immune to the influences of contraction and cutting

5. Raelin (1985) also argues that the varied organizational bases of professional autonomy have a significant bearing on the work of the manager.

6. That fact might lead one to hypothesize that the hands-off treatment was transitory. These employees may have been buffered because, as the "miracle" division that would pull American Security Bank out of crisis conditions, SystemsGroup was given the resources to expand. And, indeed, follow-up research in 1987 indicated that the work of programmers and systems people was under much greater pressure. In late 1986 SystemsGroup officials established a policy that they would no longer accept independent requests for new projects from throughout the bank. SystemsGroup research would stick with a comparatively small handful of important projects determined by higher levels of management. There was also a freeze on hiring both permanent and contract programmers.

common to other sectors of the bank. An important point through which strategic management attempted to exert control over the wage package was the enforcement of the new management methodologies. In contrast to the employees in the comparatively defenseless branch system, computer operations employees possessed a significant degree of autonomy and bargaining power on the line (not in the sense of the formal bargaining power held by unionized workers, but in the sense of labor market leverage) that shaped Systems-Group managers' responses to the new corporate agenda.

Playing with the Ranking Rules

One of the principal ways of managing the division's wage bill was to monitor salary increases and promotions by enforcing the ranking scheme. And in this task area group managers were not only subject to constraints but were also the agents of the new climate of austerity and centralization. In SystemsGroup, divisional-level management and human resources compensation personnel were pushing managers to use the ranking procedure as a tool for keeping salaries within guidelines and for managing out project-group employees at the lower end of a normal curve.

The group systems, or middle manager, was therefore at a pressure point between project groups and their output, on the one hand, and strategic management's new restructuring agenda with its potentially disruptive micro-level management techniques, on the other. Managers at the group systems level negotiated between project managers and corporate policies transmitted by the human resources staff.

Project managers pressured group systems managers against using strict ranking curves to evaluate and compensate employees. They felt that reasonably high rankings and eventual merit increases, which depended on high rankings, were critical for sustaining commitment to and integrity of the ongoing research or development project. The allegedly meritocratic purposes to which ranking (on a normal curve) was applied would, in project managers' opinions, have the opposite effect. The ranking system could not take account of important but often unmeasurable distinctions and hierarchies that were a natural "property" of these programming groups.

Project managers met quarterly with their group systems manager to participate in the process of ranking Systems-Group employees. Group systems and project managers described the lengthy, acrimonious meetings in which project managers argued to maintain relatively high rankings for their project workers. The difficulties were confounded by the fact that ranking was not applied only to one project group; all employees of the groups that one middle-level systems manager managed were merged and ranked together in one pool. Group systems managers could end by ranking dozens of employees into a bell curve if all their project-group members were consolidated.

That was one of the disruptive consequences of leaving gaps at the group-systems-management level. When more project managers were lumped under the jurisdiction of fewer group systems managers, the conflicts between different projects to be ranked increased exponentially. A wider span of control for managers intensified the politics of downsizing and contraction, which were the antecedents of ranking procedures.

One by one, each employee was ranked within his or her grade after group discussion and comparison. An employee's status might be clear, but frequently it was not; that employee would become the subject of further evaluation.[7] Stuart Milton described the process:

> I meet with the other project managers and our boss. I don't even know all the other people. It's very hard to rank; the jobs in each project group are real different.

7. In interviews, managers and systems people repeatedly referred to the process as very political; from the perspective of one nonmanagerial employee the pressure to rank and negotiate over one's employees was part of the "bloodbath" politics of middle management.

The problem is in the merging process: each manager tends to fight for their people. The second level manager has to act as a referee and come up with an equitable distribution. For pay raises or promotions, ranking makes a big difference and the bottom 15 percent are theoretically supposed to be managed out.

Hugh MacDonald's description of the merging and ranking procedure as being "like comparing apples and oranges" aptly summarized the difficulty, for both project and group systems managers, in finding adequate bases of comparison for project employees.

Another set of concerns shaped group systems managers' actions in those situations. Because they were to contain the total wage package, group managers were under pressure to get project managers to downrank or depress the mobility of their employees. Divisional-level management was evaluating middle managers on their ability, in one group manager's words, to "slow down the process of advancing people's salaries," referring not only to total dollar amounts but to numbers of promotions.

Ben Maxwell, who managed three project groups, reflected on strategic management's intentions behind the emphasis on merging and ranking. He argued that

Top management has been telling us that we're overbloated with "unnecessary" employees, that some people don't belong here in the bank anymore. They want to force the issue by getting employees to perform better or to leave the bank. They're trying to do this by getting us to whack at the bottom of our people. So they make us throw all our people into one big pool and rank them with their peers.

Group systems managers, then, had to steer the course between two opposing forces within SystemsGroup. They were pressured from the upper ranks of the division to pull wage costs into line using methods that reduced project managers' room for maneuvering and controlling project groups; methods for determining compensation that gave little credit to the particular work processes, assignments, and efforts of the many different project groups. And from below, they faced project managers' opposition to the ranking procedures of the new regime of austerity.

The opposition to ranking was a result not of innate managerial goodwill but of managers' awareness of the everpresent opportunities for mobility available to programmers and systems analysts. Why should programmers and analysts stick around when they were assured of higher salaries and regular promotions at other companies? That situation, in managers' eyes, limited their ability to use arbitrary management methods. In other words, ranking strictly on a normal curve had potentially severe consequences when it came to sustaining employees' willingness to stick with projects and the bank itself.

There was yet another way in which the new climate of decreased mobility shaped the struggle over ranking. The compensation personnel encouraged group managers to substitute one-time-only "excellence awards" for permanent wage increases or promotions. These awards had been instituted by Wedgewood as part of the new "pay-for-performance" ethic. Generous financial awards were periodically given to employees who had made significant progress in their jobs, who formulated cost-saving reorganization ideas, or who were consistently top performers.

Excellence awards could be an important motivator and indeed were viewed by nonmanagerial employees as desirable and prestigious. Project managers agreed that the awards were useful as motivators, but they also felt that in some cases the emphasis on distributing one-time-only awards was an attempt to displace the more fundamental and enduring incentive of an increased wage package. The award was an attempt to placate employees, to offset the absence of the regular and significant compensation of wage increases and job mobility.

Thus during the ranking process managers were often in

the position of bargaining against the relatively cosmetic performance award and for an improved position on the ranking list. As one project manager commented, the "performance award throws good money after a bad idea" rather than encouraging long-term outstanding work performance.

The tension in the process led group systems managers to organize an activity in which managers circumvented ranking by "playing games with the ranking numbers" and "marketing promotions." In this activity middle managers stayed within the terrain of austerity, but they reworked it in such a way that they did not force a crisis of control and consent in the production environment of SystemsGroup. Reranking games allowed middle managers to maximize the possibilities for ongoing consent to SystemsGroup goals and to juggle the competing and often contradictory demands facing them. Middle managers also protected their managerial jurisdiction by employing "management judgment," which emerged as an active ideological ingredient in strategic management's corporate culture recipe.

Playing with the ranking numbers involved two levels of activity. After determining where employees currently fell on a normal curve, group systems and project managers evaluated the previous ranking session: Who received what raises, promotions, and positions on the curve? Past positions on the curve were then weighed against present positions. Case by case, managers would redistribute employees along the curve: for example, they would shift to a higher position employees who technically were not eligible for a pay increase because of a lower position on the ranked curve but whom managers felt should receive a motivational pay increase. This maneuver entailed depressing the position of others who had received pay increases at the last evaluation session. Managers thus ranked down valuable employees, but not far enough to penalize them.

Reranking served not only to motivate employees who failed to come in at the top of the curve but also to upgrade employees, so that they were not continually categorized as poor performers. If an employee fell on the bottom 15 percent of the curve in the current evaluation period but had a higher position on the curve in the last period, managers used the positive indicator from past work performance as leverage for not managing the employee out.

By playing with the ranking rules, managers shifted employees across evaluation periods and across project groups to achieve a more equitable distribution of raises and promotions. The reranking game protected project managers from having to manage out those in a disadvantaged position on the normal curve. It was based on intense negotiations between first and second levels of management to bring the ranking system into line with the practical constraints of SystemsGroup production.

Reranking, then, allowed middle managers more room for maneuvering with project group managers; within the steadily rationalizing terrain of their jobs, they conformed to the new rules for controlling wage costs. Moreover, acting on the logic of maintaining commitments to productivity and output, middle managers refrained from shortsighted disciplinary action that would, in their eyes, have irreparable long-term costs and consequences.

In the systematic reranking process, group systems managers were working against the newly constructed and comparatively arbitrary definition of poor performers. The normalizing tool of the curve meant that any manager would always, in all circumstances, have employees who should technically be managed out. Reranking allowed managers to re-create the record on employee performance to avoid managing out.

Reranking clearly had its own set of tensions. For one thing, it often had the effect of playing project managers off one another. The ascendancy of one project manager's employee was obviously purchased with the demotion of another manager's employee. In addition, the criteria for redistributing people along the curve were frequently subjective and murky, requiring extensive discussions of dynamics and qualifications that were highly unique to individual groups. Ben Maxwell claimed:

> It often boils down to what managers can argue more persuasively. It hits an area of real subjectivity for managers and forces managers to deal very intensely with each and every employee, and with their peer and superordinate managers. But at the same time we really have to fight because ranking feeds into the reward process.

Group systems managers ran into further conflict with *their* managers. Frank Cosgrove had to convince his superior that particular employees were critical in project groups even if they had been ranked down. Ranking down could not become the basis for future downranking; the curve became something to guard and justify, to manipulate at the next evaluation session. Frank felt that it was the responsibility of the division manager to figure out why ranking procedures might be out of line—why no real norm had emerged from this supposedly standardized process. About his manager's reaction to the ranking sessions, Frank said, "My manager has to convince senior managers that all people are key even if they are ranked down. We all know there is a formal and an informal organization, and the senior people have to respect the limitations of *our* informal organization. At my level (the group systems level) complaints trickle up."

Lynn Yee went further in defending her prerogative in the ranking process. When challenged by her manager on the way she ranked her two project groups, Lynn defended her decision-making processes and insisted that he spend some time with the project groups to acquire a fuller sense of group work, project members' contributions to it, and the problems of punitive ranking in that context. She wanted him to have to confront the consequences of the ranking procedure for her employees.

Playing with the rules of ranking was a reaction against the potentially demoralizing effects of the ranking system. It is important to note that group managers were able to foster this activity because no one was challenging the ranking process in a more systematic way. Playing games with ranking served the ultimate purpose of legitimating the new regime of diminishing mobility and salary opportunities. Group and project managers' collaboration in alternating the employees who would receive raises forced them to justify and preserve the new, allegedly meritorious, arrangement.

Group managers actually used the ranking curve as a source of control over project managers, inducing their participation in reranking by suggesting the threat of a worse outcome if project managers did not go along with the game. Implicitly, if project managers refused to play, the consequences for their employees could be severe. In turn, project managers' consent to this "strategy of control" stemmed from the fact that group systems managers protected the project manager and the project group whose existence was the lifeblood of the project manager. By organizing ranking games, group systems managers created an uneasy web of interdependence between themselves and their project groups.

Because the production processes of SystemsGroup were not characterized by a systematic and extensive course of centralization and rationalization (compared with the branch system), and because of the critical function of SystemsGroup in the reconfiguration of American Security Bank, group systems managers possessed more latitude for maneuvering against the rigid implementation of new management methodologies. Group systems managers were in a better position to negotiate the employment conditions of employees whose turnover would have great costs to project life and thus to the mission of the division.

That relative autonomy may explain the nature of efforts to control middle management in this sector. Whereas in the branch system the middle management position was in the process of being eliminated, in SystemsGroup the effort to restructure management was more fragmented. It did not dismantle the middle managerial position; rather it aimed to circumscribe the autonomy of certain aspects of middle managers' jobs.

In a very different production setting, examined in the next chapter, middle-level managers were actually extended greater discretion to conduct and carry out the operations of their division. The middle managers in American Security's credit card division used this discretion not only to defend their managerial prerogatives but to redefine new productivity objectives.

6

Where Credit Is Due: Reorganizing Production in the Card Center

Strategic management's failure to invest in technology was grimly apparent in the production areas of American Security Bank's credit card center. The card center was located in an enormous urban building that was both unattractive and uninspiring. It was divided into two functional parts, one devoted to handling all merchant transactions and the other to handling individual cardholder transactions. In a white-collar production setting, the center's different work units fielded customer and merchant inquiries about accounts, approved card numbers and transaction amounts, handled merchant and customer chargebacks, developed new credit products, and "batch processed" all transaction paperwork.

As various managers guided me through their work areas, explaining the organization of work flow and the larger production process of which their units were part, I was profoundly struck by the contrast between popular images of automated, postindustrial, information-based work environments and what lay before me. Work areas throughout the center, although their individual functions were different, contained the same rows of desks, all stacked with mountains of paper. Workers sat in enormous, noisy, and distracting rooms surrounded by file cabinets and storage boxes. Not even simple sound-absorbing partitions were used to divide workers from one another.

In only a few cases had computer terminals been introduced to retrieve information. It was as though this production area were frozen in a period of rationalization that more closely approximated Mills's (1951) paper-intensive and factory-like office settings (the "enormous file") than any ideal vision of information handling in a postindustrial economy. (See Howard [1985] for a discussion of American corporate management's vision of the computerized "brave new workplace.")

When I first began my research, strategic management had just turned its attention to the card center as a profit center. To be sure, the credit card division had always been an important source of revenue (recall from Chapter 2 that, nationwide, American Security had had a very successful credit card program for many years). Historically, credit was one of the bank's "commodities"; but the new economic and industrial conditions heightened its importance as a source of profit. Thus, as the bank experienced simultaneous profit crises and struggles to maintain market share, the credit card division took on new significance in the overall performance of the bank.

Gradually, these labor-intensive production sites were transformed by computerized systems, which contained all cardholder, merchant, and bank information, storing it electronically and making it readily accessible to those who had to retrieve, report on, and summarize it. But the new systems provided more than easy access to information: they also provided new means of centralized control. New technologies could monitor workers better, using centralized telephone systems to audit phone calls in order to evaluate service representatives' ability to solve problems. The new systems could time calls, keep track of how long customers were on hold and how many hung up before being answered, and measure the number and accuracy of the keystrokes made by those who entered data for customer accounts.

Automating the production processes was one prong of

strategic management's effort to restructure the card center. In contrast to their policies toward management in other divisions in the bank, strategic management brought a new level of management to the card center. The new section heads were given carte blanche, as one of the ten card center managers I interviewed described it to me, to rectify the enormous organizational and management problems of the center. Their mission was thus quite specifically to facilitate change. They were to rationalize the currently unautomated production processes and to assist in ushering in new automated information management systems and work stations to rationalize the diverse labor processes of the card center and subject them to centralized forms of control.

One reason that the division head and members of strategic management installed new management to design new work processes, instead of simply relying on engineers, was that the engineering "experts" had met with significant resistance from supervisors while trying to rationalize and reorganize their work areas. Len Cordova, who worked as a section head on the merchant side of the card center, explained supervisors' resistance to industrial engineers:

> The staff [engineers] had to look to the line supervisors to teach them everything. They couldn't really learn the process; they had their own timelines restricting them. They [staff] had to have everything checked off by the line managers and then the staff could only pass on their recommendations. And, on top of it, their recommendations often weren't that great.

The specialists had failed to make an enduring dent in the organization of the card center's labor processes. As outsiders, they had not gained the support of line managers and made only a minimal impression with their recommendations. In part, then, the installation of a new level of management was an attempt to gain supervisors' trust and overcome their resistances to reorganizing different production contexts.

On their own, the line supervisors themselves had very little time to "innovate," as Len put it. They were under tremendous pressure to begin increasing productivity; the center was swarming with efficiency groups and external consultants who were hired to evaluate the card center work and management processes. It was in this context that a new level of middle management was put in place. New section managers were to manage a "quick turnaround" of the center, to make sure new systems would meet specific production demands. Divisional-level management made this commitment in the belief that the new managers, located in work units on a quasi-permanent basis, stood a greater chance of being integrated into the management structure and therefore would possess greater legitimacy to act as agents for the larger restructuring agenda.

Thus the new level of middle management had a very explicit role in the transition to a newly organized credit card division. Not only would they monitor supervisors and workers under them and communicate between higher divisional management and the line; they would actively seek ways to reorganize the labor process, both in its current unautomated and its future automated versions. This mission lent them a significant degree of autonomy with which to shape the course of a new productivity regime. It especially gave them a basis on which to reject more coercive aspects of that regime. Their rejection was strengthened significantly because the negative side of past growth strategies—the total neglect of technology and organization in the card center—limited strategic management's credibility in gaining managers' consent to applying coercive norms.

Card Center Managers and Managing Change

Like other middle managers, managers in the card center were critical of strategic management's role in shaping the current disarray of their division. They had a very clear view of how the turnaround task before them was adversely affected by the inadequate investment strategies of the past.

But managers in the credit card unit had a different position in the new corporate agenda. Recruited by strategic management to participate in the overhaul of the center, these managers had an autonomy from which they could set limits on certain demands emerging from the restructuring process. When card center managers were pressured to raise the productivity bar and to use higher production levels as a justification for managing out, they responded by wielding their discretion to their own ends—to increase productivity within a different set of parameters. Because they believed that productivity problems originated in labor-process conditions rather than in workers themselves, they used their knowledge about the work process of their units, past management practices, and strategic management's decision making to fend off intense speedups.

When Ralph Holstein began managing the customer-inquiry-filing unit on the cardholder side of the center, his manager recommended that Ralph push the supervisor below him to manage out several file clerks in low-grade positions. Ralph's filing unit created files, kept track of files, and retrieved them in response to customer inquiries about credit card accounts. File-tracking was separate from the actual work of answering phones to handle the inquiries; file clerks' work was set in motion by requests from customer representatives. The area was extremely paper-intensive, and access to the files was far from routinized.

When Ralph first took this managing assignment his employees could find only 70 percent of the files they needed at any given time. To give a sense of the proportion of this operation, in the three months before our interview, 140,000 files had been created, all of which were kept in metal file cabinets and cardboard boxes. Because of minimal organization in this unit, there was no system to indicate where a file had gone once it was removed, and employees could not effectively track the file and ensure its replacement. Several of the clerks in the unit had received low rankings and were perceived as slow and inefficient, an impediment to intensified productivity goals.

In Ralph's perception, the chaos of the existing labor process imposed insurmountable limitations on the productivity of the clerks. A high level of employee anxiety worsened this chaos. Many of Ralph's employees were worried about the effects of what he called the "aggressive move toward automation" on their jobs. He blamed the way the unit had been managed in the past for much of this chaos. Employees had been unwillingly subjected to the disorganized character of the card center, he argued; a manager was justified in working to manage them up to higher productivity levels.

In his position of reorganizing the labor process without computerized systems to handle the file documentation and retrieval electronically, Ralph's first major project had been to systematize the filing procedures so that clerks would have ready access to any given file or, if the file had been drawn, would know precisely where it was.

Ralph's innovation was at once a dramatic improvement with respect to the existing system and startlingly simple with respect to organizational sophistication. Under the new system, clerks replaced files with one-page forms on which the name and account number of the file, the name of the clerk withdrawing it, and the date of withdrawal would all be recorded. These forms thus provided information about the location of the file; under the old system the whereabouts of a file had remained a mystery until it was replaced.

The new system raised the accuracy of retrieval from 70 to 90 percent and simultaneously increased the productivity of the clerks. Ralph was also generating productivity statistics that had never before been maintained. These statistics were used to manage up employees. He was gradually transferring all information on work flow and output—information on numbers of inquiries, the types of files being pulled, the number of files different departments were bringing in per day, week, and month—to a small computer; tallies of the information would be made available to employees. He called the old system, under which no one had up-to-date information on production activities, a hit-or-miss system inadequate to the rapidly changing production environment.

That managers use statistics on employee work activities to monitor, control, and manage employees may seem a most obvious and even insidious truth to students of the labor process. Typically, workplace observers consider primarily the negative implications of such detailed monitoring procedures for workers. Under the conditions described in this study, however, in which middle managers were challenged to raise productivity levels and maintain some degree of consent to ongoing productivity objectives in the context of restructuring, I would argue that managers used such statistics to set limits on the degree to which workers could be pushed, from higher up in the corporation, to achieve new productivity levels. Ralph was devising a system for ultimately managing up the production employees over whom he held responsibility; but he maneuvered this system in opposition to more extreme demands, from higher divisional-level management, for increasing productivity and getting rid of employees who could not reach greatly increased production levels.

While Ralph turned his attention to innovating the existing organization of work in the file unit, he simultaneously protected his own prerogative for managing his employees. The lack of a viable way to measure productivity under the old file system further strengthened Ralph's ability to generate new productivity statistics that conformed to the changing labor process and the relevant constraints on productivity. He simultaneously opposed demands from higher levels of the division for productivity and staff reductions.

Diane Timbers was a "master" at manipulating numbers and variables to maintain control over her unit of customer service representatives. The seventy representatives, whom she managed through five managers, spent their time plugged into IBM PCs and headphones, answering questions about credit card accounts. A firm believer in the idea that numbers enabled workers to define and participate in achieving productivity goals, Diane's weapon of management was a massive statistical volume in which she documented multiple bases of productivity. She had systematically generated numbers on all aspects of staffing, such as number of full- and part-time employees, classified by hours worked, productivity, grades, ranks, and salaries; customer inquiries, stratified by credit products, type of credit inquiry, number of complaints, and marketing costs; and productivity measures such as the number of incoming and outgoing telephone calls, their length, and resolution time frames.

Diane had been brought in to do "systems enhancement": to find better ways to organize this particular customer inquiry unit. Before Diane's arrival the "reps" had worked two to a terminal. Now each rep had his or her own PC. (The reps were predominantly, but not solely, women.) One of her pet projects was to help design new screens for the inquiry process that would enable the reps to solve customer problems better.

The level of uncertainty in the work of these employees was staggering. The rules and regulations pertaining to credit cards changed continually as new credit products were introduced and chargeback time frames and procedures changed. Customer service jobs had a six-month learning curve in which reps attended about ten hours of training sessions a month to familiarize themselves with handling the 3,000 to 5,000 daily customer inquiries.

Diane had hired two extra supervisors to juggle the demands of what she described as a "fast-paced environment." In addition to managing the work flow, supervisors were actively involved in handling calls that representatives could not resolve. Thus Diane was plugging in staffing gaps, using supervisors to increase the general productivity of the unit.

Despite the complex and increasing work load incurred as more cardholders were brought into the bank's card program, divisional-level management made several specific demands for higher productivity in Diane's unit. For example, one of the objectives written into a recent PPCE was that Diane would manage an overall reduction in the costs of the unit's phone calls and therefore in the amount of time it took her representatives to resolve customer inquiries. Ostensibly, that objective meant that she and her supervisors would pressure their employees to speed up their telephone transactions, with the ultimate goal of reducing the number of representatives needed to staff the unit.

As it turned out, the costs of her unit's calls increased in that period. It did so, however, because of the addition of a new phone system in the unit, a fact that Diane was able to establish through detailed calculations of a variance analysis. That system, an automatic call distributor, more efficiently and rapidly forwarded phone calls to the numerous representatives. By factoring in the costs of the new phone system, as well as giving the reasons for maintaining current staffing levels (which she was able to justify with her stratified measures of incoming calls and types of calls as a result of new credit products), Diane was able to justify the total telephone costs incurred in the period. She used an elaborate set of equations because, in her words, she refused to have her unit penalized for what she saw as an "arbitrary intervention," wherein someone, somewhere higher in the division decided on a new area of cost cutting.

In that particular case she used the numbers to argue on her own behalf with her manager about what was and was not possible with regard to cutting both costs and staff. More to the point, Diane used those production numbers to protect her unit against the confusion surrounding the installation of new technology systems. Her statistical manipulations allowed her to invalidate new demands by showing how her work area was negatively affected by the new systems.

Diane viewed the new concept of managing out as similarly arbitrary. In her view, employees who fell on the bottom 15 percent of the ranked curves performed their jobs quite adequately. She also insisted that "managers want to manage up. It's in our interests to get people to perform better. Managing out is only a solution if managing up doesn't work."

Diane claimed that it was critical to set boundaries on what higher-level management could squeeze from those production areas. Their attention was only focused on profitability, without considering the negative and undermining implications of heavy-handed approaches to achieving profitability. "Top management now sees the card center as very profitable. But in terms of the care they're taking for our long-run success in pushing through new programs it's like we're living hand-to-mouth. If the unit can make profits top management wants us to make even more profits."

Sarah Fleischman saw the entire card center as completely out of control, a state stemming from past neglect of automation and productivity standards. As a section head on the merchant side of the center, Sarah managed six supervisors and through them seventy indirect reports. Her unit processed chargebacks: whenever a cardholder or cardholder's bank disputed a charge made by American Security's participating merchants, the amount was charged as a debit to American's account until proper liability had been established and American Security had been cleared of the charge. It is worth looking at this particular unit in some detail, for it reveals the pressure of processing information in an environment in which every second funds are unaccounted for is a drain on company profits.

For the period during which a chargeback was unresolved, the bank was liable for the figure under dispute and lost the additional interest that would accumulate on that amount. In this extremely labor-intensive production process the bank's risk of high and uncontrolled losses ran higher the longer it took to account for these debits.

The employees in Sarah's unit adjusted claims as soon as a customer disputed the account. Their role was to document and investigate each claim meticulously. They obtained both the draft of the account from "file builders" in another unit and documentation from the cardholder about why the charge was disputed. The adjuster was to consider all aspects of the dispute and make a decision about proper bank action.

Any number of factors could cause a customer to initiate the chargeback process. A cardholder's name might appear on a "Warning Bulletin" listing individuals prohibited from using their credit cards: if the merchant did not refer to the bulletin but nonetheless accepted a customer's card, the cardholder's bank could challenge American Security's charge. Or a merchant might claim they had billed a cardholder for an order placed over the phone, although the cardholder denied placing the order.

Whatever the nature of the dispute, it was the responsibility of the file adjuster to provide accurate data for settling the case, optimally in favor of American Security, by removing the charge from the liability column. When Sarah entered this position in early 1985, the unit had an enormous backlog of chargebacks. The rows of adjusters' desks stacked high with photocopies of documentation at every stage of every account under investigation were vivid testimony to the lack of effective measures for both "capturing money" and "capturing data."

Sarah had been promoted to section head to facilitate this chargeback unit's transition to an automated environment. She noted that in some locations, on the cardholder side of the center, employees were able to bring up customer accounts handily onto a terminal screen for quick responses to inquiries; on her side, however, terminals and PCs had not yet been introduced. She claimed that "Mr. 'X' [the past CEO] wouldn't approve a budget for investing in new technologies in the card center. He also wouldn't go outside American Security Bank for software. It was a situation where things were left alone and management didn't deal with these issues." When she took on her large chargeback unit she found it very difficult to get it to move: "When I first came people didn't know quite how to measure things. Managers hadn't known how to do budgets or any kind of staff forecasting. They didn't have time to step back and ask how can this be done better. I inherited a very messy situation."

By eliminating some duplication of cross-referencing pro-

cedures and by instituting measures that enabled the chargeback unit to reduce the error ratio from 20 to 5 percent, she
felt that she could move the unit beyond the enormous backlog of accounts to be resolved.

Nevertheless, she had been given new quotas for increasing
volume and decreasing staff that were, in her view, "no good."
In response to these projections she wrote a staffing and planning forecast that was more realistically aligned with the
current capacities of the chargeback unit, factoring in new
productivity potentials resulting from the preliminary reorganization strategies she and her supervisors had introduced.

Sarah's role as a representative for corporate change was
enacted within parameters she developed about how to negotiate the existing inadequacies of the labor process with new
pressures for productivity. Her philosophy was in distinct opposition to the philosophy of "opaque management," in which
managers cajole workers to do something on the basis of individualistic concepts such as achieving one's personal potential through stretching, rather than because of the stark facts
of pressures for corporate change. One manager liked it, she
said,

> Because I tell them [workers and managers] what's going
> on, what the rationale is for what they're doing. I don't
> just say "do this," or try to hide from them the political
> and economic pressures on our work. You need to ex-
> plain or people don't get what's going on. Downward
> communication is very important. In this situation there's
> lots of political pressure, there are a lot of people leaning
> on us; it's especially bad when the bank is experiencing
> these bad losses.

Like Diane and Ralph, Sarah summoned the expertise she
had gathered in her unit and managed her supervisors and
workers within a different set of standards from those proposed by divisional-level management. She simultaneously
used her leverage to manage divisional-level demands and to

press for cooperation from those in the chargeback unit. In this sense, frank and open management was a form of persuasion and manipulation that served Sarah's role in maneuvering the unit toward higher productivity levels. She gained some degree of legitimacy from her oppositional position to top management, which she used to further her own aims in the production unit.

These managers undertook their mission with the belief that it was the organization of the labor process, rather than individuals themselves, that was responsible for productivity deficiencies. In reorganizing the labor process they worked to manage people up to new productivity levels. However, there were important limits to their view that the organization of the labor process alone was to blame for the lack of productivity. Managers in the card center felt strongly that workers and supervisors had to understand and cooperate in the demands for reorganization that were pressuring everyone. As the branch managers attempted to get branch employees to participate in increasing productivity, the card center managers tried to use their numbers to buttress their position vis-à-vis workers as well as divisional-level management. Ralph, for example, summarized and organized, in a central terminal, the productivity figures for his supervisor's filing unit so that workers themselves could develop a baseline standard for new achievements.

Diane's adamant posture on having comprehensive and accurate figures with which to guide her unit to new productivity levels was reflected as well in her belief that workers must take more responsibility for meeting higher goals in the unit. For this reason, she posted productivity figures, for the unit as well as for individuals, on a wall for all to see. She used her aggressive position vis-à-vis strategic management to strengthen her latitude with her employees. Her open-office policy and her ability to summon the data necessary to command her unit were weapons in winning the cooperation of her supervisors and their employees. Diane's opinion of employees' responsibility for their fate in the future of the card center reflected her unwillingness to bear the full brunt of responsibility:

> I post the standards daily for the reps to see. The reps want to know what they are being measured against. Performance shouldn't be a mystery! The employees here have to make the choice about whether or not they want to be managed up. We give them that choice but they have to run with it. And frankness is the only way to deal with it, that's how we can decide if the employee is ultimately good for the job or not. It may be that there is a skills mismatch and that some kind of lateral mobility is the answer.

Those examples in which managers used computerized reports to accumulate statistics on output and productivity run counter to claims that computers inevitably deskill managers. In the card center, managers generated reports for divisional-level management and their employees to protect their units and their autonomy in decision making. Whereas numbers and reports stood as weapons for the expropriation of expertise from branch managers, numbers and reports were weapons of autonomous management in the card center.

Because of the different position held by the card center in the bank's restructuring agenda, higher-level management was limited in its ability to push or coerce those managers. Compared with its treatment of the branch system, strategic management had taken a hands-off approach to card center production sites, giving hands-on authority to managers to control and to initiate changes. Thus middle managers were given the authority to make restructuring decisions within their production sites. In the branch system, on the other hand, authority for restructuring decisions was external to production sites and was held, not by middle-level production managers, but by area management groups and the strategic-management-level policy team that was uniformly and by fiat organizing the reduction of branches.

Finally, this hands-off approach gave card center middle

managers more room to protect themselves with their criticisms of strategic management for past strategies—specifically, the failure to update and automate the labor- and paper-intensive work processes. Strategic management recognized its own past policy deficiencies and sought the cooperation of middle managers to transform this large and potentially very profitable production unit. Under these conditions, middle managers' arena of discretion was actually enlarged, whereas in SystemsGroup discretion was circumscribed and in the branch system it was expropriated.

The new level of management in American Security Bank's credit card center was ushering in the corporate restructuring processes, but in a gradual way, so as to increase productivity within the constraints of existing labor process conditions. We could conjecture that strategic management's ultimate vision of the card center was of a work site that, once automated, would operate with far fewer supervisors and middle-level managers. The new technological systems, with their potential for centralized control, could ideally minimize the need for direct supervision and higher-level coordination of production groups. In this sense these managers might, in the long run, be managing themselves out of positions by reorganizing and preparing different work sites for new technologies. Indeed, Len Cordova speculated that the section head level of management was transitional: "They [section head managers] are there to speed up the conversion process. They make sure the controls are in place as new processes are instituted. Middle management may then be phased out."

At the same time, there may be limits to such an ideal picture, insofar as it underestimates the role of middle managers in coordinating workers and supervisors to use materials, machines, and time. When I asked Diane whether and how managers were necessary in her case, where workers were plugged into centrally controlled terminals, she responded, "The monitor may give numbers but numbers achievement depends on people and coordination. Also, you can have all the data in the world but you need someone to make sense of them. And I spend a lot of time on the floor. I have to be there to fight fires."

By 1987, middle managers had acquired an even larger role in negotiating between the ongoing productivity of work sites and new technological systems. Len Cordova had by that time been promoted to managing four "cost centers" on the merchant side of the center and was indirectly managing sixty-five employees. He described how strategic management's attempts to catch up rapidly to state-of-the-art systems and rectify decades of neglect had had a whole new set of unforeseen costs. Major systems glitches had occurred. The inability of units to assimilate all aspects of the new technologies had led to significant losses of electronically captured data, and thus to real monetary losses, and there was much uncertainty about the best strategies for setting the center on a more stable and routine automated track.[1] The possibility of eliminating managers seemed remote at that point. Although strategic management may have viewed the new level of management as transitional, middle managers seemed to have been thrust into an even more critical role in staying a long course of conversion.

Conclusion

Labor-process theorists may find nothing remarkable about the conclusions drawn in the last three chapters. Middle man-

1. See Adler (1986) for an excellent discussion of the unanticipated and exorbitant costs of rushing ahead with new technologies to "deskill" the work force. He calls this strategic perspective the "myth of deskilling," the idea held by top managements that new generations of equipment will permit reductions in skill requirements and therefore labor costs. Instead, rushing to install new technologies can lead to "costly realignments of personnel profiles" for the firm (Adler 1986, p. 13). For similar reasons Bolwijn and Kumpe (1986) note that top managements must take precautions before introducing the technological components of new flexible manufacturing systems. The introduction of flexible specialization systems is not exclusively a technological issue, they argue; flexible manufacturing also demands a retooling of the social relations between labor and management on the shop floor.

agers deploy their discretion to achieve certain corporate ends. They attempt to draw workers and other managers into intensified efforts to increase productivity. Those claims may provide ample proof of a one-sided view in which middle managers willfully execute restructuring, possessing a predictable set of interests by which they manage, in tandem with top management, in the coercive corporate interest.

Examining middle managers working within different production contexts and facing different sets of constraints demonstrates how, in fact, middle managers' actions were shaped by an alternative sense of the corporate interest. American Security's managers contested the ways that strategic management's new corporate policies would make workers and managers pay the costs of both past and present policies. Middle managers refused to execute important facets of the new managerial agenda, such as ranking, arbitrarily raising productivity bars, and obscuring the import of centralization and contraction, tools that would coercively cut the numbers of employees in the firm and alter a historically paternalistic set of employment policies.

Nor does the dispute over means constitute evidence of the irrationality of middle managers, their self-interest in historically accumulated power, or their fear of conflict, as many management theoreticians and consultants have been quick to claim. It is, rather, evidence of a logical response to the constraints that different levels of managers faced in the form of production politics and resources, for which no quick or superficial turnaround solution exists. It is also evidence of a strong rationality, insofar as middle managers perceived that their actions had the power, at the simplest level, to keep operations running.

Managers rejected top management's particular definition of entrepreneurial management—using their judgment to downsize the firm—but they did use their judgment extensively to reshape their own workplaces. Whether innovating group work processes (as in the branch system), measurement and evaluation (as in SystemsGroup), or the production process itself (as in the card center), middle managers ac-

tively wielded their expertise in a set of oppositional management practices, both to organize the consent and cooperation
of employees in their units to achieve long-term productivity
objectives and to defend their units from the coercive aspects
of the new agenda.

A one-sided interpretation of middle management fails to
consider the autonomy and expertise lodged in the ranks of
middle levels of managers and thus cannot adequately com-
prehend the limitations of top management's control over
middle managers. Nor does it ask how managers organize
production (specifically, within what constraints middle
managers must maneuver) or how managers organize cooperation and consent. This study suggests that middle managers cannot be seen solely as agents of capital and top management and that the terrain on which managers organize
consent may become a terrain of struggle within corporate
management. It also suggests, contrary to the notion that
managers resist simply to protect their turf or to stave off any
kind of change, that managers undertake change, but it is not
necessarily of the sort that top managers desire. Further,
managers may have substantial reasons for refusing to manage out their own functional expertise.

Middle managers' capacity to respond to the new agenda
differed according to "sectoral differentiation" (Baron and
Bielby 1980), details of which are summarized in Table 1. The
branch sector was being dramatically transformed: as production processes and the control over them were rationalized and externalized, the domain of middle managers' responses was restricted to struggling within the branch to
organize existing resources and personnel. Because branch
managers' control over ranking processes had been centralized, the tool of ranking did not become an object of struggle
as it did in SystemsGroup. Branch managers' efforts were thus
devoted almost exclusively to organizing and mobilizing
branch employees.

Card center managers similarly worked to reorganize
and mobilize workers to higher productivity. Card center

Table 1. *Summary of Management Restructuring in Three Production Contexts*

| Variables | Organizational Location | | |
	Branch System	SystemsGroup	Card Center
Strategic importance of division	Contraction	Holding the line	Expansion
Status of middle management	(−) Elimination of branch manager position. Removal of operational, personnel, innovation management.	(+/−) Standardizing and controlling decision-making process of group systems managers.	(+) New line of management inserted. Section heads given greater authority (especially innovation and operational management).
Status of production processes	All levels of work in branch are being centralized; some automation. Large cuts in branch system.	Project/programming work not centralized, standardized. Wage packages being contained.	Production processes being automated, although not centralized.
Sources of middle manager autonomy	(−) Branch managers' knowledge. How to reorganize branch workers to meet new constraints.	(+/−) Critical function of research and development. Labor market conditions, autonomy, skill.	(+) Section heads possess superior knowledge of production constraints and ability to generate and analyze numbers, production reports. Comparatively hands-off approach.
Forces of centralization/ rationalization	Area management group. "Retail Action Team."	Human resources group and organizational centralization.	Automation experts.
Domain of response	Efforts focused on managing up, preserving branch; branch managers lack ability to oppose criteria of divisional management (defensive).	Efforts focused on protecting project managers' role in managing project groups. Intensified vertical negotiation.	Efforts focused on managing people up, but according to criteria opposed to those of divisional-level management (offensive).

managers, however, resorted to offensive strategies, unlike the defensive actions of branch managers; they protected their jurisdiction as managers and in turn used their ability to maintain autonomous positions with respect to divisional-level management as a weapon for eliciting cooperation from card center employees. These managers controlled the productivity numbers and used them to forge an even more autonomous vantage point for managing.

Part of that strategy revolved around one critical variable: discretion over production-process innovation and production decisions had been moved from branch managers' jurisdiction to area management, whereas it had been enlarged for card center managers. Branch changes were imposed from outside the branch unit and were of a comparatively unequivocal nature. In the card center, section managers dictated the course of organizational change, acting on the autonomy of their new position and their knowledge of production processes. The organizational space in which to defend autonomous management practices was therefore different in these areas. Whereas branch managers' negotiations were centered on their own work sites, card center managers' negotiations were vertical, directed toward higher levels of management.

One more critical variable is needed to explain the ability to protect autonomous management: the functional importance of the different areas. Strategic management targeted the credit card center as an increasingly significant profit center, whereas it targeted the branch system as a less significant source of bank profitability. Profitability considerations per se did not affect group systems managers in SystemsGroup. SystemsGroup's functional role in the restructured bank was, like that of the card center, a critical one. But even in SystemsGroup—a research and development division that in noncrisis conditions may have been immune to cost cutting, rationalization, and centralization—the autonomy and decision-making processes of middle managers themselves were targeted for greater control. For SystemsGroup managers the evaluation and compensation process became the domain of struggle.

Like the card center managers, SystemsGroup managers had a degree of leverage for organizing consent and cooperation, but they did not have a role in reorganizing production, and they lacked detailed productivity figures to fend off top management and elicit consent from below. Measurements of actual SystemsGroup output were minimal compared with the measurable work processes of the card center. But the main target in SystemsGroup was the total wage bill of the division, and ranking was a primary mechanism for slowing down wage increases and eliminating allegedly superfluous workers. We can best understand group systems managers' interests in reranking as a response to being targeted as the agent for cutting the wage bill.

In part, managers' resistance was based on efficiency considerations. They were under scrutiny themselves, and their ability to achieve new productivity quotas depended on whether they would be capable of gaining consent to new objectives. Their concerns for increasing productivity, however, were tempered by a set of considerations about consent and about past and present conditions of the workplace that strategic management would have preferred to ignore.

In this regard, middle managers' resistance to the coercive aspects of the new agenda even benefited workers in the restructuring process. Some may want to argue, in contrast, that the ways in which managers managed, documented in the foregoing three chapters, simply evidence coercion and not protection of workers. Inducing workers to throw their weight behind *middle managers'* objectives obviously involved some degree of manipulation, a manipulation made all the more inequitable by the fact the relationship between managers and the managed was fundamentally inegalitarian. But managers' oppositional practices, and their effects on workers, had a decidedly more complex character. The point is not that managers were, or even necessarily perceived themselves as, the humane arbiters of corporate change. Rather, in defending their own domain of expertise, to further their particular vision of what best served the corporate interest (a vision that included a unique interpretation of the social relations of the workplace), managers also defended workers from the more extreme aspects of strategic management's productivity and downsizing demands.

Strategic management's vision of middle managers as the agents of their own demise and of the downgrading of their employees neglected a simple and real fact: these managers played a critical role in organizing other managers and workers to achieve productivity objectives, and top management faced severe constraints in turning that relationship on its head. Middle managers do not simply collect and process information up and down the management hierarchy; nor are they a mechanical apparatus of control that simply and mysteriously makes employees conform to rules and regulations.

My research thus challenges another orthodoxy about American middle management: the notion that middle managers can be automated out of existence as their "information processing" function is absorbed into computerized systems. They play a legitimating role, combining technical and social relational expertise; it is they who must absorb the contradictions of restructuring, and they deploy their unique knowledge about specific production sites to do so.

Managers' resistance was not only pragmatic. It was political, in that managers were angry about strategic management's handing them a set of tasks that could not compensate for the real and fundamental problems of the firm. Their belief that layoffs should be initiated (even knowing their own positions could be in peril); that top management's failure to modernize the firm and invest in certain technologies had hurt the firm's prospects for profitability; that strategic management was adopting Band-Aid policies by forcing all managers to attend "corporate culture" training, were all ingredients of an anti-strategic-management politics. In that politics, although middle and strategic managements may share a vision of corporate objectives, significant differences exist over the appropriate means for achieving these ends.

The specific content of coercive autonomy revolved around the attempt to deploy managerial discretion to the goal of corporate downsizing and restructuring and a new regime of intensified productivity and savings. Strategic management could order managers to manage out as a form of disguised cutbacks, but the micro-level execution of techniques to achieve cutbacks resisted precise specification or rationalization. Middle managers consequently were exhorted to take more aggressive action, to use their managerial judgment in an autonomous fashion. Nevertheless, as we have seen, the exercise of judgment, innovation, and entrepreneurial behavior were subjected to strict surveillance.

In proffering the strategy of coercive autonomy, strategic management was proposing a new solution to a historically variable problem: managing management, or managing the domain of action that rests between the firm's need for centralized control (necessary because of increased size and complexity) and its need to extend discretion (necessary because of the imperative to delegate authority) (Bendix 1956, p. 336). Under the particular conditions of profit squeeze, contraction, and restructuring, top management both scrutinized and exploited discretion in a historically unprecedented way.

But discretion is not an autonomous capacity that workers or managers carry around with them to exercise uniformly in any production context. Rather, discretion is shaped and developed within specific work contexts; it is valuable because it is developed as a "way of knowing" over time. Thus discretion cannot be codified. Furthermore, production processes and relations at the lower levels of the firm cannot be arbitrarily and abstractly manipulated without regard to prior organizational practices. In American Security Bank, middle managers toiled not merely to preserve traditional practices but to build on established practices to create the conditions for a renewed corporation. This is certainly one dimension of the corporate interest that remains undertheorized.

In the corporate agendas that emerged in the 1970s and the 1980s, corporate leaders would ideally use middle managers to transform the employment and production structures of contemporary American industry. In the current international context of competition and contraction, however, many of the real solutions to profitability rest in more fundamental and enduring restructuring policies. In an important way, strategic managements are facing the consequences of decades of specific capital-maximization strategies.

Whether or not top managers will accept the responsibility for these consequences remains open. American Security's strategic managers attempted to decentralize and obscure the responsibility for remedying one of the major problems of the bank. But middle managers' criticism of strategic management ultimately forced top management to adopt more direct, visible means for downsizing and cutting back. Strategic management's failure to gain managers' compliance to absorb the costs of restructuring was evidenced in the progression of events over 1986 and early 1987.

By 1986 there had been little significant reduction in the ranks of American Security Bank's employees. Reductions proceeded very slowly; reports indicated that only 8,000 employees left the bank over a four–five-year period as a result of the combined forces of redeployment, normal attrition rates, the sale of company assets, and retirement. Much speculation circulated about strategic management's failure to scale down American's operations dramatically. Some commentators even suggested that Wedgewood was constitutionally incapable of taking deep cuts in the corporation.

In fact, Wedgewood attempted something quite bold by banking on the thousands of managers below him to get rid of allegedly superfluous employees. Wedgewood and his top committee threw their weight behind the "managing up or out" strategy, behind culturally reforming the managerial style to be more productive and aggressive.

Those broad reform efforts were overshadowed by the bank's mounting loan losses. Strategic management was forced to bolster American Security's loan loss reserves, thus lessening profits. Even the sale of properties and entire subsidiaries to reduce the effect of profit loss through one-time capital gains failed to halt declining earnings.

American Security's situation was further complicated when the Federal Reserve Board and the Comptroller of the Currency stepped up their intervention in American's affairs.[2] As a result of pressure from federal agencies, American Security was unable to use lending as a growth tool. The regulators refused to allow American Security Bank to expand loans on its equity base, ordering strategic management instead to redirect capital into building the equity base and loan loss reserves to a higher level, protecting the bank and bank depositors against accumulating losses.

Even more significant, the Comptroller pressured American Security Bank to reclassify many more loans as "nonperforming," resulting in increasing loan write-offs. Spurred by earlier bank collapses, federal authorities targeted American Security early on as potentially troubled. Its basic core of deposits and good loans were viewed as solid, but the breadth

2. The federal authorities possess significant power to rectify a troubled bank. They can pressure a bank to discontinue paying dividends to shareholders if they believe such payment jeopardizes the bank's economic health. As another form of intervention into the bank's profitability, federal authorities can force strategic management to reclassify loans. The Comptroller can insist that strategic management remove key individuals in the upper ranks of the bank, if it believes that such persons are not taking sufficient steps to stave off decline. The experience of Continental Illinois is a case in point: when Continental deteriorated, the Federal Reserve Board, the Federal Deposit Insurance Corporation, the Comptroller's office, and a consortium of twenty-four banks (providing financial assistance) collaborated on an interim program to save the bank. The program called for a massive capital infusion, appointing new members to senior management, and asking the entire board of directors to resign (Miller 1985). As Horowitz (1986) points out, federal regulators had an immense stake in preventing Continental's collapse, as they do with any major U.S. banking institution (pp. 157–160).

of American Security's financial influence meant that all authorities were on alert for damaging economic effects of the loan losses.

Finally, after months of public and private skepticism about the quality of American's management, the board of directors came under intense pressure to make a change in strategic management, whether the effect was symbolic or real. Wedgewood left the bank in the mid-1980s.

After his departure, strategic management was forced to announce that they would quickly undertake widespread layoffs of up to 5,000 employees. Regional newspapers carried front-page headlines about the future layoffs, and less than a year later, strategic management reported that they had in fact exceeded the originally anticipated reductions. They had aimed, in that one-year period, to cut staff by 5,000 and had eliminated over 6,000.

There is evidence, although unofficial, that even here American Security's strategic management did not directly cut thousands of workers from its payroll. Projections of future cuts notwithstanding, actual large layoffs apparently never materialized. According to the banking correspondent for the regional newspaper, much of the attrition at American Security Bank resulted from the combined effects of the fear of layoffs and the active promotion by the bank of a severance package. Significant numbers of employees had been driven to take advantage of the package rather than wait for notice that their position would be eliminated.[3]

Managers' resistance to managing out did not cause this eventual outcome. In other words, just as middle managers' practices cannot be blamed for American Security Bank's decline in the early 1980s (despite strategic management's attempts to scapegoat middle management as the major im-

---

3. Personal communication with the banking correspondent. This information was confirmed by local television coverage of the firm (which added that when employees accepted the severance package, they signed contracts relieving the firm of legal liability in future lawsuits).

pediment to productivity and competitiveness), neither can their responses to the corporate restructuring processes be blamed for the more recent dramatic events of the bank: asset sales, vast scaleback of its operations, large profit losses. Their reactions did, however, have an important constraining effect on the domain of top management action. By refusing to accept responsibility for what they perceived as an unjust and inviable agenda, American Security's middle managers eventually forced strategic management to take greater and more direct responsibility for the painful task of restructuring its own labor force.

7

Reconstructing the American Workplace

Over the past fifteen years, corporate America has undertaken a dramatic and wrenching restructuring: deindustrialization, corporate downsizing, and extensive takeovers, mergers, and acquisition activities dominated the corporate profitability strategies of the 1970s and 1980s. Previous chapters have illustrated, in addition, how firms devoted significant resources to transforming their employee relations frameworks and their internal cultures in trying to cut costs and prepare workers for leaner times.

Still to be determined is how best to reassemble the pieces of American industry left behind by these strategies. What will corporate structures and work processes look like in the 1990s and beyond? And what are the links between restructuring the American workplace and restructuring management?

These questions hold vast economic, organizational, and cultural implications, and a surprising consensus about their answers has emerged among corporate leaders and a new generation of postindustrial theorists. The new consensus for reconstructing the American corporation rests, above all else, on criticism of rigid bureaucracies and the belief in flexible production processes. Stepping back from the case-study material to examine this consensus, this chapter will generalize from the experiences of American Security Bank to show how "productive flexibility," when appropriated by corporations and directed at the work of managerial and nonmanagerial employees, may cause fundamental changes in the organization and authority relations of management.

Although the notion is necessarily speculative, I wish to suggest that American Security Bank's commitment to creating managerial "flexibility" while simultaneously reconfiguring its middle management ranks echoes a larger trend toward change in the bureaucratic management apparatus that has been the mainstay of large American corporations throughout the twentieth century. Coupled with the ideological and structural reforms discussed in earlier chapters, the popular consensus for productive flexibility provides the remaining piece of a very large and complex puzzle about contemporary changes in American middle management.

The Argument for Productive Flexibility

In a recent and influential book, Cohen and Zysman (1987) survey the economic context of the 1980s and 1990s and argue that the increasingly competitive environment of these decades has and will continue to put inescapable pressures on the production processes and relations of large U.S. firms. In their view, large corporations will have greater difficulty dominating market niches over a long and stable period; therefore, corporations must create the organizational capacity to respond quickly and flexibly to new, often short-lived market demands. Cohen and Zysman claim in particular that managers must enhance the capacity for innovation close to the line, giving greater responsibility to workers with hands-on skill and knowledge.

Focusing on the breakup of mass markets and the inability of the large American corporation to respond effectively to an era of slow economic growth, other industrial policy analysts have taken up the argument for more flexible innovative capacity (Reich 1983; Piore and Sabel 1984; Walton and Lawrence 1985). If the United States is to regain its stature as a major industrial competitor, according to these authors, large firms must be able to respond quickly to direct market—hence continually fluctuating and competitive—pressures. Not only should flexible production characterize our remaining manufacturing or industrial enterprises but firms producing services should also encourage flexibility in the way services are delivered (Hirschhorn 1988).

These postindustrialists also argue that every member of the industrial community should play a part in restructuring the corporation. Top managements may need to redesign corporate strategies; but workers and lower levels of management must be willing to redesign their work methods and relations. A body of literature on the postindustrial labor process focuses on worker responsibility, autonomy, and self-management, suggesting that the contemporary workplace be reconfigured along the lines of "neo-Fordism" (Sabel 1982), "postindustrial work systems" (Hirschhorn 1984), and "flexible specialization" (Piore and Sabel 1984).

If workers can overcome their reliance on rigid work rules and antagonistic postures toward management, if they commit themselves to continually learning and developing new skills and to performing job tasks interchangeably, they can contribute to a historical shift in American productivity and production relations. In the current context of global competition, these policy analysts argue, neither workers or managers can afford any longer to gloss over workers' expertise or dismiss workers' potential to perform as responsible, autonomous producers.

Further up the workplace hierarchy, middle managers and supervisors should redistribute their authority and place greater faith in "high-trust" relations with workers; in so doing, they will unblock a tremendous reserve of worker skill, enthusiasm, and commitment (Sabel 1982).[1] Eliminating tradi-

1. Curiously enough, this same observation was made in the early 1970s in the HEW report *Work in America* (1973). However, whereas

tional hierarchical distinctions between workers and managers, based on the historical centralization of knowledge in the hands of management and engineers, is thus seen as a critical dimension of moving the American economy into a new competitive age.

To gain the participation of workers and managers in such change, these theorists charge, employers must offer basic guarantees of job security to establish workers' commitments to more flexible, participative, and specialized production processes.[2] Reich (1983), for example, calls for U.S. firms to guard the nation's "human capital," emphasizing that workers should not be penalized for the restructuring of industry; while Cohen and Zysman (1987) deliver an impassioned plea to employers to initiate skills retraining for workers, rather than resort to skill and job displacement through the use of new technologies and offshore production.

Ironically then, the visions of corporate management (discussed in Chapter 1) and progressive public policy analysts converge on the goal of dismantling the bureaucratic management structure. In reflecting on the possibility of a less hierarchical workplace, the postindustrial theorists argue that operational and personnel authority, historically lodged in corporate middle management and supervisorial levels, must be passed down to work teams that are self-managing. The bureaucratically administered organization of operations and personnel management may have been adequate for expansion in a stable, growth-based economic context, but the very system of coordination and administration that helped make American corporations prosperous will, according to the post-

---

in the 1980s work reorganization was advocated to improve American business competitiveness, in the 1970s it was advocated to rectify pervasive worker alienation. (Improving productivity was seen as a not unimportant by-product of reducing alienation.) The HEW task force argued that alienation arose from the inadequacies of the Taylorist organization of the work process, a more highly educated work force, and changing cultural values regarding the meaning of work.

2. Such a dual commitment underlies what Walton and Lawrence (1985) call a mutualistic human relations framework: the "commitment human resources management system."

industrial perspective, undercut their ability to maintain a competitive footing in the world economy. For the postindustrialists, the current economic crisis—and its organizational determinants in the bureaucratic American corporation—is a case of the chickens coming home to roost: large employers must now pay the cost of management systems that have typically robbed workers of skill, responsibility and discretion.[3]

The plans for flexible production systems, put forth by those determined to renew American competitiveness, depend on a new system of management. That system entails a diminished role for middle managers, with operational and personnel responsibilities centrally coordinated by higher levels within the corporation and with an increase in responsibility for those working on the line. By using an array of organizational and technological instruments designed to promote flexibility, American employers will be able to decrease the organizational distance between the upper and lower reaches of the corporation. In the movement toward this new system, the fates of managerial and nonmanagerial workers alike are intertwined in the changing corporate division of labor; changes in one strata shape changes in the other.

Four corporate trends currently capitalize on the call for productive flexibility. By far the most important of those trends is the implementation of worker-participation schemes in the American workplace, followed by the increasing use of contingent workers, computerization, and the use of centralized management groups. Furthering the effort to mitigate hierarchies and rigidity, all four are converging to transform the work and position of middle managers by allowing top levels of management to coordinate, direct, and control production processes without their aid.

Although they are ostensibly promoted in the name of flexibility, those trends obscure two issues. The first is the way

3. Holland (1989) documents this orientation and its consequences in meticulous detail in a recent study of the rise and fall of a machine-tooling firm.

that flexibility serves the firm but not necessarily the interests of the parties who are principally affected, workers and managers. The second issue is the way flexibility undermines the historical role of middle managers in corporations.

New Ways of Working:
Some Implications for Management

With a new emphasis on participation, top management has been trying to draw both blue-collar and white-collar employees into taking more responsibility for production in unionized and nonunionized firms. Estimates of the extent of worker-participation schemes vary, but there is no doubt that they are widespread and have increased significantly in the last decade. Wells (1987), for example, argues that one-third to one-half of the Fortune 500 firms have some version of "quality of work life" (QWL) schemes, and Lawler and Mohrman (1985) claim that over 90 percent of the largest Fortune 500 firms had quality circles by 1985. A 1982 New York Stock Exchange survey found that quality circles were the fastest growing human resource programs in U.S. corporations with 500 or more employees (cited in Drago 1988). Using a different unit of analysis, Kochan, Katz, and McKersie (1986) report that employee-participation schemes affect about one-quarter of the work force (p. 213).[4]

In U.S. collective bargaining in the 1980s there has been a surge of negotiations related to implementing QWL and employee-involvement programs, following decades in which labor and management leaders paid lip service to such con-

4. See *Businessweek's* (10 July 1989) recent feature story for an informative and updated assessment of top managements' motivation to install worker-management participation programs. Giving a precise figure on exactly how many programs are in use is complicated by the problem of defining and classifying the numerous participative schemes. Quality circles, job rotation and enlargement, and autonomous work groups all come under the rubric of participative programs for workers. The general preoccupation with worker involvement is evident, however.

cepts (Freeman and Medoff 1984). Firms have attempted to give workers more voice and have encouraged managers to respond positively to heightened worker involvement on the shop floor (Freeman and Medoff 1984, pp. 248–249), efforts top managements now see as mandatory to improve U.S. economic competitiveness.

By bending previously inflexible work rules, encouraging quality circles and QWL programs, and enlarging workers' responsibility and authority levels—all policies that coincide with the postindustrial perspective on flexibility—business leaders can turn workers into managers and minimize the firm's dependence on middle levels of management to arbitrate production. Top managers and work experts laud this model as the wave of the future; consequently, the ideology and cultural discourse of decentralized, autonomous management has been ladled out to production and manufacturing workers as well as to managers themselves.[5]

Semi-autonomous work groups in a firm, many business leaders and postindustrialists argue, can make production decisions more quickly if they can bypass the centralized decision-making processes of higher levels of managers. Such groups can be given authority to set up and maintain machinery, keep track of inventory, order materials, document production costs, and participate in budgeting and forecasting. Walton and Lawrence (1985), advocates of workers' participation, argue that workers need to become involved in all operational and personnel decision-making areas, including quality control, short-term planning and monitoring of product flows, selection and training of new employees, and daily trouble-shooting activities (p. 355). While plant management develops the broader goals, workers develop their own

5. See Hodgetts, Lawrence, and Schlesinger (1985) for an informative case study account of the way this model of work and the ideology of self-management and flexibility on which it is based have been implemented in a trucking firm. Parker and Slaughter (1988) also present a series of illuminating vignettes, cases in which the "team concept" was introduced.

skills and competencies with support from trainers and team advisors (Beer and Spector 1985, p. 228).

It is important to remember that reshaping workers' roles along these lines is strongly associated with corresponding changes in the role of middle managers. One of the significant repercussions of an expanded role for workers has been the "total elimination of one or more entire levels in the traditional hierarchies to remove redundancies and shorten communication lines" (Walton and Lawrence 1985, pp. 355–356). In particular, the self-managing team approach, in which workers redesign their own jobs, take responsibility for quality control and output, and work comparatively autonomously, leads in many cases to the elimination of middle levels of managerial workers (Hall and Isabella 1985; Sherwood 1988), which in turn increases flexibility on the shop floor and allows the firm to quickly respond to changing market conditions.

This interactive process, wherein managers' and workers' jobs are reshaped with the advent of participation schemes, occurs in a variety of industries. Studying a chemical company undergoing restructuring processes as a result of international competitive pressures, Nichols and Beynon (1977) show how the enrichment of workers' jobs directly correlated with the demise of manager and foremen positions. "Self-supervision" and the addition of responsibilities to workers' jobs mainly involved workers in absorbing the tasks and the costs of elimination of managerial positions (Nichols and Beynon 1977, chap. 4).

The example of the white-collar bank teller in American Security Bank's branch system demonstrates the interactive dynamic between the empowerment of lower-level workers and the eventual displacement of management. The bank promoted some tellers to corporate officers with the effect of reclassifying tellers as supervisors and enlarging their decision-making capacities about a variety of branch issues. That reclassification process also had the long-run outcome of eliminating branch managers from the superbranches. What appeared to be an increase in flexibility and added responsibility for bank tellers was part and parcel of a decrease in responsibility and authority for branch managers. In sum, changes in the middle management function in American Security Bank were predicated on, indeed would have been impossible without, changes in lower-level branch occupations.

This "multi-occupational" process means that changes in one occupation interrelate with the transformation of other occupations within a diversity of workplaces. That is, deskilling an occupation or a function may entail upgrading or creating another separate occupation (Reskin and Roos 1987; Baran and Teegarden 1987). A perspective that spans the multiple functions of an organization is crucial for understanding shifting patterns of skill and authority relations. Firms are not only transforming the *occupation* of management, they are transforming the *system* and *organization* of management. Examining the overall organizational context of deskilling and upgrading is thus important for understanding contemporary occupational change (Simpson 1989).

When companies introduce worker self-management schemes, middle managers find themselves acting as agents, yet being the targets of change. According to Bradley and Hill's (1987) study of the implementation of quality circles in ten companies, the burden of operationalizing participative management often falls directly on middle managers. Bradley and Hill (1987) argue that managers view their role in setting up quality circles as "add[ing] to managerial workloads for comparatively small returns" (p. 75); but at the same time managers have to manage out their own positions as they hand over decision-making powers to workers. Because managers lose power as responsibility is shifted down to lower-level workers, there is often a great deal of confusion in managers' roles when participative schemes are introduced (Schlesinger and Oshry 1984; Simmons and Mares 1985, chap. 13; Manz and Sims 1987). Simmons and Mares (1985) found that as corporate management urges rank-and-file workers to take more and more responsibility, and urges both workers and managers to adhere to new philosophies of self-management, middle managers "fear the possibility that they are being asked to participate themselves out of a job" (p. 221).[6]

The current reordering of the way production is managed—of the essential tasks involved in overseeing productive processes and work relations—raises the historical importance of workers as agents in the management structure. No doubt workers have always overtly or covertly played a significant role in directing production. Indeed, nearly the entire corpus of industrial sociology addresses the role that workers play in directing production, whether informally, through the restriction of norms and regulation of work groups, or formally through collective bargaining procedures. Corporate management, however, is explicitly drawing out this role in the competitive environment of the 1980s and beyond. Workers not only should produce, but should be vested with authority to employ their unique expertise in the service of production objectives.

Although it is by no means new, interest in this participative ethic has a prominent role in current strategies for improving the performance of U.S. industry. The current emphasis on participation, coupled with real structural changes, is aimed at reorganizing the contemporary management hierarchy in a very different way from earlier approaches to involving workers in workplace objectives, such as the human relations framework. In other words, worker participation and responsibility is the other side of the "demanagerialization" of the workplace, a process that was unfolding in American Security Bank's branch system during the period of this study.

A second trend ostensibly promoting flexibility leads to a

6. Reports of irrational managerial resistance to ushering in participation schemes thus have to be analyzed in these particular contexts. If managers understand that they are managing themselves out of a job or that they will be evaluated on production outcomes without having control over how those outcomes are achieved, they may well resist in various ways (Berg, Freedman, and Freeman 1978).

fundamental transformation of management. In an attempt to reduce fixed labor costs and make employment itself more flexible (Freedman 1988; Osterman 1988; Pfeffer and Baron 1988) many businesses are cutting back permanent, full-time employees, replacing them with temporary, part-time workers. The Bureau of National Affairs (1986) recently reported a significant increase in the corporate use of nonmanagerial part-time, temporary, flex-time, and seasonal workers. The authors of the report explain that this increase is a result not only of the rise of a service sector of employment but also of corporate top management's perspective that full-time permanent work forces have become a liability to "maximizing productivity and minimizing costs" (Bureau of National Affairs 1986, p. 2).

As the manager of labor law for the U.S. Chamber of Commerce comments, work forces made up solely of permanent employees "tend to handcuff the employer in a time when there is a revolution in the workplace" (Bureau of National Affairs 1986, p. 3). This revolution is now a permanent feature of the workplace: employers must be able to institutionalize flexible employment conditions in order to adjust their work forces in the context of a highly competitive and fluctuating economy. The authors estimate that a contingent work force of part-time, flexible, temporary, and seasonal workers now numbers over 28 million workers—one quarter of the U.S. work force—who will be the first to lose their jobs in periods of corporate contraction.[7]

---

7. Others have confirmed that corporations use temporary employees—clerical, professional, engineering, and managerial—in order to go "lean and mean" on a moment's notice (Carey and Hazelbaker 1986; John 1987; Freedman 1988). Aside from being the first to go in economic downturn, these workers face the added disadvantages of relatively poor compensation, fewer health and medical benefits, overall lack of job security, and lack of opportunity for career development (Pfeffer and Baron 1988, p. 297). All of these are typical of the conditions that women and minority part-time, temporary, and seasonal workers in secondary labor markets have faced for decades (Smith 1983).

This trend reconfigures management on two levels. Increasingly, in a way that many observers feel is unprecedented, managers are being made peripheral in the same way as workers. Firms use displaced managers as a flexible, "contingent" labor force, contracting out their managerial responsibilities. Predicting a growth in a "two-tier" work force, much like the two-tier wage structures that companies have used to privilege long-term workers and disadvantage newer hires, the *Wall Street Journal* (4 May 1987) claims that firms will dismiss tens of thousands of managers from their permanent core employment activities, who will then become part of the peripheral, temporary, self-employed tier of managers that firms hire only when needed.

Supporting these hypotheses, one commentator argues that despite the Bureau of Labor Statistics' optimistic projection of managerial employment through the 1990s,[8] many firms will hire private managerial subcontractors who take temporary management positions, once held by permanently employed middle managers in large companies. These subcontractors will account for much of the projected increase of 20 percent or more in the managerial and executive category (*Fortune*, 2 February 1987; see also *Wall Street Journal*, 4 May 1987). And increasing numbers of companies also have insisted that managers shift from full-time to part-time work schedules in response to budget cuts and increased financial pressures (*Wall Street Journal*, 2 June 1982).

The explanation for the peripheralization of management is economic in part and pertains to nonmanagerial employees as well: if they can organize more of their managerial work force on a temporary basis, firms can respond to economic

8. The Bureau of Labor Statistics projects that employment in the managerial and executive category will increase 22 percent by 1995, compared with a 15-percent growth rate in total employment (Silvestri and Lukasiewicz 1985). This general pattern is consistent with Wright and Martin's (1987) observation that over the 1970s there was an acceleration of the rate of expansion of managerial-class positions within nearly all economic sectors in the United States.

fluctuation readily, sloughing off redundant employees in slack times. This second trend also converges with the first, participative, trend: an integration of managerial tasks into workers' jobs and decreasing dependence on managers. As workers take on more managerial responsibilities, firms can displace regular managerial employees.

The move to peripheralize both managerial and nonmanagerial work forces has perhaps even greater consequences for the structure of management. When firms reduce the core of permanent, full-time, committed employees and increase the periphery of temporary part-time floating employees, they externalize formerly internal costs and functions (Mangum, Mayall, and Nelson 1985; Pfeffer and Baron 1988). The consequences for managers can be unprecedented and unpredictable. Although it will undoubtedly create new managerial problems and specializations (in particular, it raises the prospect of having to manage across different organizational boundaries), the externalization of functions can also shift management tasks outside the corporation to temporary agencies and other subcontractors and thus reduce the number of critical functions to manage within the large corporation (Pfeffer and Baron 1988, p. 294). Further, if externalization of employees and functions reduces the size of a division or a manager's span of control, managers' compensation and prestige may be affected (p. 295).

Osterman argues that "the increasing use of temporary workers can be viewed as an effort to transform . . . the occupation in question from one involving stable internal employment with an element of job security and training to (from the firm's perspective) a hire/fire relationship with no commitment" (Osterman 1988, p. 63). This shift, in turn, leads to changes in managerial work. As more firms move that objective to the center of their strategic agenda, more and more middle managers, much like those in American Security Bank, may find themselves thrust into the unenviable position of mediators and targets of ongoing corporate change.

Computerization of both production processes and management functions, seen in American Security's branch system and credit card center, represents the third trend that may lead to centralized control with greater responsibility discharged at the lower levels of the corporation: the technological capacity to displace managers and decrease the organizational distance between top management and production work. Computerization of production processes frequently has a positive effect on both manufacturing and white-collar occupations, leading to expanded tasks and responsibilities. At the same time, however, computers can be used to decrease the discretion and autonomy of certain levels of management. Top managements have introduced computer networks that integrate plants and divisions with corporate levels of the firm. Integrated systems give those at the top direct access to production-process data bases, thereby enabling top managers to bypass the judgment of middle levels of production managers and to use their access to the data to manage managers (Zuboff 1988, chap. 9). The ultimate outcome is the displacement of some levels of management (Osterman 1988, p. 78).

When computers are introduced into bottom-level work processes, they affect processes further up the corporate hierarchy as well. Computerization leads to greater productivity for the clerical work force, decreasing the need for supervisors and managers as it decreases the need for many clerical workers. In addition, computers have the power and range to monitor workers, a task typically performed by managers. And as blue-collar workers become more involved with flexible technologies, they take over functions previously performed by such white-collar professional and managerial workers as production planners and inventory control staff (Osterman 1988, p. 78).

Similarly, as insurance companies computerize data-entry and underwriting functions, they create new jobs that combine managerial and professional, service, and clerical responsibilities into one workstation or labor process (at the same time wiping out both the most routinized clerical jobs and a higher level of managerial jobs). Combining those functions leads to the expansion of new job categories (Baran and Teegarden 1987, pp. 210–212) that can be classified as managerial. Even if turning workers into supervisors represents little more than job inflation (Reskin and Roos 1987), those cases are important for understanding the symbolic and the real ways in which management tasks are being redistributed throughout organizations.

A fourth trend that enhances comparatively centralized systems of management in the name of flexibility is organizational: the heightened use of centralized personnel groups in a changing workplace. Kochan and Capelli (1984) argue that in the context of the competitive economic environment of the 1980s and the ongoing decline of the labor movement, corporations are giving centralized personnel groups greater prominence and power in order to mediate and control new problems of labor management.

> It is clear that the distinction between labor relations, human resource management, and operating management will become increasingly blurred as firms attempt simultaneously to control production costs, increase employee communications and involvement, maintain stable union-management relations where unions exist, and avoid new opportunities for union organizing.
>
> 1984, pp. 154–155

As in the new organizational arrangement of human resources staff in American Security's SystemsGroup, centralized personnel groups may acquire more and more of the responsibilities of middle managers. Top management at American Security touted the new system as a way to decentralize human resources management and make it more responsive to diverse divisional concerns; in fact, the system created a more direct and centralized line of authority between the SystemsGroup unit and top management. In general, centralized groups are assuming new and authoritative positions in the corporate management circuit.[9]

9. See Ferris, Schellenberg, and Zammuto (1984) for corroboration of such a renewed role for human resources personnel as industries face conditions of decline and contraction.

The concentrated management structure, part of the concept of area management (Chapter 4), will similarly decrease the organizational distance between strategic management and production processes. The area management group would allow the spatial reorganization of middle management (a form of off-site management), as AMG representatives would circulate about branches, monitoring and evaluating branch employees.

Observing the convergence of these four trends, we may reasonably ask whether we are simply witnessing a return to the craft-like, autonomous work processes that characterized an earlier form of management predicated on a high level of decentralization of shop-floor production processes. If we were to accept the claims about flexible manufacturing at face value we could almost envision the reemergence of a simple drive structure of management, in which workers semi-autonomously worked on their own with only a loose system of management, "unintegrated" in Litterer's (1963) terms.

The "drive system" preceded technical and bureaucratic management systems (Nelson 1975). A comparatively decentralized arrangement consisting of integrated knowledge and control held by those directly involved in production, it included foremen as the most immediate representatives of strategic management (Gardner and Whyte 1945; Roethlisberger 1945; Wray 1949; Patten 1968). The drive system of managing production also included some degree of workers' participation in coordinating and directing the work process.

Before the rise of coordinated, bureaucratic administration, discussed in Chapter 1, firms were vulnerable to market exigencies. The drive system "allowed for flexible adjustment to shifts in demand and was effective in holding down unit labor costs" (Jacoby 1985, p. 123). To maximize profitability, firms had to be able to respond to external factors outside their control; they were sensitive to and confined by local markets, suppliers of materials, and agents of distribution (Edwards 1979, p. 24). The drive system thus allowed firms to maintain a short-term manufacturing orientation (Jacoby

1985). Foremen and plant managers, administering employment in a variable and unpredictable economic environment,
"looked for quick results and maximum flexibility; the work
force was to be adjusted to changes in technology and to fluctuations in output" (Jacoby 1985, p. 6).

That description does not stray far from the vision of the
proponents of flexibility. But is the early twentieth-century
structure of management appropriate for the contemporary
corporation? Sophisticated organizational and technological
devices as well as the profound shift in employment practices, all discussed above, give corporations far more power
to control, monitor, and integrate low-level production activities. Although firms may encourage workers, supervisors, and
middle managers to embrace the ethos of participation, the
fact is that participation, increasing responsibility, and decision making all occur within an environment under tight surveillance. By slashing levels of management; strengthening
and legitimating their ability to cast off superfluous workers
and managers; increasing their ability to gain detailed data
immediately about production, distribution, and finance by
means of computer systems; and relying on centralized, high-
level managerial groups, top managements decrease their organizational distance from production operations and solid-
ify their ability to manage from afar.

Such techniques were not available to owners and managers of the nineteenth and early twentieth century; indeed,
technical and bureaucratic management systems, introduced
in different periods of the twentieth century, were deployed
precisely to overcome the extensive autonomy enjoyed by
workers and supervisors under the early drive system (Edwards 1979). Thus more likely than a return to the earlier
system is the emergence of a new form of work and management with only the semblance of decentralization: the responsibilities of middle-level management pushed down into
the lowest levels of the corporation, and workers increasingly
prevailed on to act both as workers and managers within

tightly defined limits. (See Burawoy and Lukács [1989] for a similar criticism of the flexible specialization thesis.)

In sum, what may seem to well-intentioned policy analysts to be humane and logical reorganization strategies often represent to corporate top management little more than license to institutionalize the impermanence of jobs and skills and thus workers. The concept of flexibility, while providing tangible benefits for employers, currently portends more troublesome results for corporate workers themselves. Clearly, managerial and nonmanagerial employees alike end by paying the costs of flexibility and corporate restructuring.

The Politics of Flexible Production

The proponents of flexibility have made many provocative claims. Sorting through the devastating restructuring processes of the seventies and eighties, these theorists are attempting to chart bold directions for corporations in the 1990s and beyond. Between the admonitions to adopt a more flexible orientation to markets and the guidelines for a more participative and flexible set of workplace relations, they have offered us the ingredients for a transformed corporate America.

Blueprints for increasing productivity and uniting the efforts of labor and management in a new corporate agenda are critical. However, they can only suggest to us what *can* be, not what *will* be. Much about the restructured postindustrial corporation, although perhaps technologically and organizationally feasible, is politically indeterminate, something rarely acknowledged in the postindustrial optimism. Because of that indeterminacy, it is important to discuss the politics of change in order to assess the likelihood of moving to new flexible, postindustrial work arrangements.

Skeptics have not held back from addressing the political difficulties of this issue in the prevailing atmosphere of dissension between labor and management in the United States. Howard (1985), for example, agrees with the thrust of the postindustrial perspective. He notes that new computer technologies, often adopted to give corporations a competitive edge, prefigure a more positive and decentralized reorganization of work that can benefit management and workers. Workers could assume greater responsibilities in organizing production and could utilize their unique skills to design new ways of working. At the same time, Howard argues, the new technologies are not likely to reveal their potential in the current antagonistic labor-relations climate of American industry, unless management agrees to treat workers as partners, with respect and trust. If current hierarchical arrangements prevail, workers will be forced into a coercive brave new workplace. In view of the current orientation of American corporate management toward short-term profit-making, Howard may be correct in his pessimism. American employers may hesitate to make the long-term investment in the technology and training necessary for implementing genuinely flexible and participative work systems. This point is only briefly touched on by Sabel (1982, p. 219) in his discussion of neo-Fordist work arrangements.[10]

Zuboff (1988) emphasizes even more adamantly that American business organizations stand at the crossroads with regard to new, flexible technologies. All too frequently, she argues, top-level managers operate under traditional restrictive assumptions about their political relations with labor. More than willing to deploy computers solely to automate (and thus to extend control over workers), management will seldom strive to maximize workers' skills and intellect or use the technol-

---

10. Even when American firms do adopt flexible manufacturing systems, they frequently use such systems in the service of rigid and centrally controlled goals (more typical of the Taylorist organization of work) than in the service of a new form of flexible production (Jaikumar 1986). A contrast to the Japanese case is instructive. Because of a thoroughly different context of industrial relations and employment policies—particularly policies of long-term employment—Japanese employers have been far more willing to invest in reskilling and training for new work arrangements (Kenney and Florida 1988, pp. 131–133).

ogy simultaneously to incorporate and expand workers' unique knowledge through what Zuboff calls "informating" processes. To take the former route will be fatal, according to Zuboff, because it will permanently consign American firms to a regressed, secondary status in the world economy.

Highly suspicious of claims about the benefits of flexible specialization for workers, Gough (1986) suggests that the new technologies that facilitate flexible specialization production systems, such as CAD and CAD/CAM (Computer-Aided Design/Computer-Aided Management) are often precisely the technologies top managers use to deskill and impose new systems of discipline on workers (Gough 1986, pp. 65–67). Workers must self-consciously and systematically develop their own "oppositional restructuring" agenda to increase the unity of the working class and enable that class to struggle effectively against capital.

Whether or not the new work arrangements can succeed must be considered in the context of prevailing labor/management politics. Middle managers themselves frequently object to coordinating worker self-management (an objection interpreted as irrational, inexplicable resistance to change in the popular business press). Cognizant of losing authority and discretion as workers are empowered, many middle managers object to passing on decision-making powers to lower-level workers when managers may still be held accountable for final outcomes. Not coincidentally, but without adequately explaining why, Lawrence (1985) sees managers' resistance to the new ethic of participation as one of the biggest blocks to the upgrading of workers' jobs (p. 359).

Workers too, in many cases, have greeted new flexible work arrangements with ambivalence and distrust, generating a highly politicized atmosphere when asked to become managers and to embrace new flexible technologies and organizational devices. Workers often view increases in responsibility without increase in compensation, heightened involvement as self-managers, and reduced participation of upper-level managers as indicators of significant speedups and future redundancies (Simmons and Mares 1985, chap. 14).[11] Such perceptions create a negative payoff to the firm when workers feel that new work arrangements and technology are a source of stressful extra work and accountability rather than a source of enrichment (Zuboff 1988).

Simmons and Mares tout the potential advantages to workers, citing the decrease in alienation and increase of morale and pride as important outcomes of greater worker involvement. Yet even they acknowledge that one of the principle limitations of existing QWL programs and other schemes designed to enhance worker participation is that in the majority of cases in which participation has increased, there has been little fundamental change in workers' power and authority. The result has been the disillusionment and antagonism of the workers. Asked to do more, to consider themselves as agents of management, and to adopt the goals of the firm as their own, workers' ability to control the most meaningful factors of work life (investment, plant closures, etc.) is nevertheless sharply circumscribed, a situation well captured in Simmons and Mares's phrase "participation but not control" (1985, chap. 7). Often management uses quality circles to give workers the "feel" of participation without a meaningful voice in decision making, or to co-opt existing and future unions with the intent of maintaining managerial flexibility (Grenier 1988; Parker and Slaughter 1988; *Businessweek*, 10 July 1989).[12]

11. In one very revealing example, the human relations director in a General Electric appliance plant, where self-directed work teams were being used to increase the plant's cost competitiveness and decrease the need for supervisorial employees, remarked that workers' greatest dissatisfaction with the new program was that they were not being properly compensated for the increased level of tasks and responsibilities (Hickey 1987). This concern was consistently expressed when Thomas (1988) interviewed aerospace and electronics workers involved with flexible technologies.

12. For other examples of workers resisting self-management schemes, see Nichols and Beynon (1977) and Liker, Roitman, and Roskies (1987). See Parker and Slaughter (1988) and Wells (1987) for excellent discussions and pessimistic assessments of the increased use of quality of working life (QWL) programs to maneuver workers

Unions have responded in various ways to flexibility. As mentioned earlier, recent collective-bargaining negotiations have included commitments to employee-involvement programs. In many cases unions have agreed to those programs because they have no options: they must either acquiesce to management's demand for flexibility or see their plants close down (Kochan, Katz, and McKersie 1986). But some unions have resisted worker-participation schemes; union leaders, for example, may resist joint consultation with management on flexible technologies and worker involvement because they fear that their members will feel they are simply being co-opted by management (Thomas 1988).[13] Indeed, the pressure to participate has occasionally backfired, leading dissident rank-and-file workers, in at least one important case, seriously to challenge the judgment of their union leadership and to call for new leaders who will be less willing to cooperate with top management.[14]

---

into taking more responsibility in the current era of increased competition. Wells (1987) argues that such programs try to "hide the supervisor in the worker's head" (p. 9).

13. See Kochan, Katz, and McKersie's (1986) discussion of union resistance to QWLs (chap. 6), and Hammer and Stern's (1986) argument about the conditions under which unions will and will not cooperate with management's participation schemes. Hoerr's (1988) study of the steel industry illustrates well the sources of organized labor's suspicions about participative schemes. In an effort to salvage the company's productivity in the 1980s, top management of LTV Corporation introduced labor/management teams in many of their plants. Despite labor's cooperation, a major plant was closed down (the Aliquippa plant) and all its workers thrown out of their jobs. Many union members felt betrayed; critical United Steel Worker's members argued that employees had effectively worked themselves out of their jobs (Hoerr 1988, pp. 155–161). On the whole, as I will discuss later, Hoerr is optimistic about participation and feels, in fact, that U.S. industry is doomed if management cannot include labor as a genuine partner in production (1988, chap. 23).

14. See, for example, the rise of the dissident faction "New Directions" in the United Auto Workers. New Directions opposes UAW leadership on the grounds that it has too readily embraced the concept of "cooperative adversary" as well as numerous "jointness" programs between management and workers in the auto industry

I do not conclude from those cases that the redistribution of managerial authority is unequivocally bad for workers. To the contrary, the outcomes for workers are indeterminate. The downward movement of authority, for example, in and of itself may have positive outcomes for workers as they gain greater control of shop or office. It may be very much in workers' interests to participate in top-down self-management schemes if, for example, the survival of the firm depends on increasing productivity. Indeed, the redistribution of authority can benefit both workers and the firm; it is known that managers can inhibit productivity by ignoring workers' unique expertise (Juravich 1985).

That indeterminacy, however, means that it is important to demystify the concept: to investigate the numerous and ambiguous causes and outcomes, for workers, of "flexibly organized production" and, in particular, to understand the interaction between and politics of managerial deskilling and worker "upskilling." It becomes important to ask, for example, who initiates flexible programs and what happens to compensation and job classifications as firms burden their workers with managerial responsibilities and eliminate strictly defined managerial positions? Will job security be guaranteed in return for the relaxing of job classifications and any subsequent productivity increases? If firms have the unstated goal of laying off workers and closing plants, then gaining the participation of workers in self-managing teams to stave off closure temporarily can rightfully be viewed with suspicion. Ironically, the unequal trade-off between top management and workers—in which workers make concessions about flexibility but gain little or no power to influence decisions concerning the security of their jobs and their firm—could limit the successful spread of so-called QWL programs, since, in the estimation of Kochan, Katz, and McKersie (1986), QWL ini-

---

(*Wall Street Journal*, 15 June 1989; J. Schwartz 1989; *Businessweek*, 10 July 1989).

tiatives stand the greatest chance of success when they are linked to employment and income security (p. 211).[15]

Demystifying flexibility is also important for understanding how restructuring may affect opportunity structures for women and minority workers. In key ways, the techniques designed to implement flexibility may diminish opportunities for women and members of other historically disadvantaged groups. In the light of the present examination of American Security Bank and of data on larger trends in the organization of employment relations, three outcomes seem possible in the coming years.

First, when firms wipe out middle managerial positions, they eliminate positions that have only recently been made available to women and minorities. The most significant change in women's labor-force patterns in recent years has been their increased participation in managerial and administrative jobs: women went from being 18.5 percent of the managerial and administrative work force in 1970 to 37.9 percent in 1987 (Blum and Smith 1988; U.S. Bureau of the Census 1989). Throughout the 1970s, black workers made important gains in professional and managerial staff jobs in large corporations, after decades of being excluded from those positions (Collins 1989). As firms become more committed to cutting overhead in the form of administrative costs and layers, they are doing away with the jobs that had just opened up to women and minorities and undermining the advances these groups have made in wages, status, and security.[16]

15. Finally, the term "flexibility" has become such an all-purpose one that it helps, to resolve the ambiguity, to take a hard look at what corporate managers mean when they use it. Capelli and McKersie (1987) found that in many cases in which employers stated their intention to "go flexible," insisting that workers go along with the breakdown of job rules and classifications, the effect was usually to eliminate restraints on *managerial* decision making, allowing management to deploy workers flexibly on its own terms (pp. 451–457).
16. See *New York Times* (4 January 1987) for an important analysis of how the corporate staff jobs many black professionals and

The computerization of workers' jobs can similarly undercut supervisorial jobs that have been important bridges for
women and minorities into the upper levels of the corporation. New integrated computer systems combine production
and supervisory tasks previously performed by different jobholders into one job at a computerized workstation. In tandem with the computer system that has the capacity to measure and control the worker using the technology, one upgraded
clerical worker runs the workstation without being directly
monitored by a supervisory worker; the new integrated jobs
are often dead-end positions even though they are comparatively upgraded (Baran and Teegarden 1987). Doing away with
bridge jobs can both keep women and minorities out of internal labor markets, which provide greater security and certainty of mobility, and weaken the internal labor market itself by taking away the progressive steps upward in the firm.
In sum, eliminating low- and mid-level managerial jobs in
the service of flexibility may systematically destroy employment opportunities only recently gained by women, blacks,
and other minorities.

Second, a countervailing trend that is part of the movement toward flexibility may have a unique effect on women's
work opportunities. As firms try to implement quality circles
and other participative schemes in blue- and white-collar

---

managers entered in the 1970s, such as public relations and Equal
Employment Opportunity positions, are precisely those that corporate managers are now cutting. In management's perception, those
positions do not contribute to bottom-line performance. In a related
and ironic development, Kanter (*New York Times*, 17 August 1987)
suggests that the current emphasis on risk taking and entrepreneurialism in corporations may block women's mobility in a new way.
More and more, she argues, reaching the upper levels of the firm
depends, not just on rising in the ranks of the company through a
stable career ladder, but on being a "star" and having a tremendous
reputation for being unusual and innovative. Many share the belief
that women and minorities have had to work harder at their jobs
just to be accepted and to be considered as talented as their male co-
workers; if Kanter is correct, this task is becoming much more bur-
densome in the age of the entrepreneur.

workplaces, they may seek employees who have great emotional flexibility and a high tolerance for intense personal relations to work as "facilitators" or "group leaders." Such persons may be perceived as being better equipped to cajole and manipulate workers and overcome their apprehensions about new technological and social work arrangements. Companies might design jobs just for those persons, who presumably would be most able to cooperate and least strictly committed to hierarchical authority relations.

If, for whatever reasons, employers view women as well suited for that type of intense, cooperative, interpersonal work, they may go to great lengths to recruit women employees for the purpose. And in fact some managers and management experts have argued that firms would do well to recruit women to work in the less hierarchical, less bureaucratic firm of the postindustrial era. Women make better managers, in this line of reasoning, because of their allegedly superior ability to cooperate, intuit and work around the feelings of others, and confront situations that are intensely social-relational (see Blum and Smith [1988, pp. 530–534] for a review of this claim).

Although this second trend would open up a sphere of managerial jobs for women, in contrast to the first, which does away with managerial jobs, the new job category could easily turn into a less desirable, "feminized" occupation. By gender-typing lower-level managerial and supervisorial jobs as "women's work," managers and employers could deliberately select women over men and exclude women from other types of positions. Psychic costs to women will be high if they are continually thrust into changing, uncertain, and fluid positions with responsibility for absorbing tension and conflict over changing roles in the workplace. The costs would also be monetary, if women are confined to a new female ghetto of relational work with the characteristic disadvantages of female occupations, such as lower pay and prestige (Reskin and Roos 1987; Strober and Arnold 1987). In other words, female managerial work could stabilize as a subspecialty within the larger occupation of management (Reskin and Roos 1987).

Cutting across the first trend of diminishing opportunities at higher levels in the firm, the expansion of intense interpersonal managerial jobs would stymie women's mobility by restricting them to a new "emotion work" ghetto (Hochschild 1983).

The issue of a feminine—hence gender-based—managerial style is provocative, but, in this case, it is a smokescreen. It obscures potentially costly and permanent changes in women's employment as a result of corporate restructuring. What is important, however, is whether and how employers exploit the theory of difference between male and female managers to justify confining women in disadvantaged positions.

Finally, the growing trend toward the peripheralization of professional and managerial jobs offers American corporations new ways to marginalize women. For decades, of course, women and minority workers have had the majority of part-time and temporary jobs, most frequently at lower levels of large firms or in the secondary labor market (Edwards 1979, chap. 9). In both situations, women's wages were among the lowest in the economy; they received few benefits and had few opportunities for promotion (Smith 1983).

Now, however, firms are employing more elite professional and managerial workers on this basis. Very likely this so-called dual internal labor market (Mangum, Mayall, and Nelson 1985), only recently emerged, will be interwoven with women's employment patterns. That is, because of family and child-care constraints and managerial stereotypes about women's lesser commitment to careers, employers may hire white male workers for core activities and women for their peripheral work force. Women may have to accept part-time and temporary jobs, even though so many women have worked in the core work force on a full-time and permanent basis over the last fifteen years.

Unfortunately, the increase of a peripheralized professional and managerial work force coincides all too well with a current corporate interest in developing different career tracks for different groups of women. These tracks vary according to managements' perceptions of whether women will be committed, long-term employees or will have a dual commitment, to a less than all encompassing professional life and to raising families. The female dual-track proposition has been described, analyzed, attacked, and defended in the popular and business press (F. Schwartz 1989; *Businessweek*, 20 March 1989). However much its advocates wish to deny that the dual track should be used to discriminate against women, the so-called mommy track already appears to firms a perfectly reasonable way to accommodate both women's needs and the needs of the firm for greater flexibility.

If firms need a peripheral work force that can be shed or built up according to prevailing economic and market conditions, top managers may well tap into a pool of workers they perceive as having only an intermittent interest in wage labor, less interest in promotions and mobility when they are employed, and weaker bargaining power—a description that closely fits Felice Schwartz's (1989) picture of the women on the family/work track. Thus alternative, non-fast-track career choices for women will be institutionalized in the unpredictable employment practices of firms.[17]

The outcomes of this trend, too, have an indeterminate, political character and will depend on a worker's class and race. For women who have the organizational bargaining power and leverage—presumably upper-managerial, educated, skilled workers in the largest corporations—these trends could prove to be emancipating. Those women will be in a better position to control when and how they will work on a part-time or temporary basis, rather than at the mercy of the corporations' business cycles.

17. The interest in a "mommy track" also clashes with the new corporate emphasis on entrepreneurialism and being a "star," in Kanter's terms (see n. 16). If mobility depends on being a star (and working on the terms that stardom requires, such as twelve- to sixteen-hour workdays, total commitment to one's work, flexibility to be at the beck and call of the firm), then both women and men who are committed to raising families will be kept from entering higher levels of management.

For other women the outcomes will be mixed. The labor-force participation of those employed by less paternalistic or less profitable firms, or those whose race, ethnicity, or lack of education casts them into a less privileged position, will be more vulnerable to uncertain business cycles. Firms must develop the capacity to respond to economic downturns and up-swings and the capacity to change product lines rapidly; firms may inflict the corresponding unpredictable employment needs of business fluctuations on disadvantaged groups of women employees. Privileged women will be in a position to control the timing of their employment and to accommodate their personal life-cycles to the business cycles of the flexible post-industrial firm without paying huge personal and professional costs. But less privileged women and women of color may be forced to accept whatever positions are offered them, regardless of the fluctuations of their own lives.[18]

Overall, restructuring and flexibility appear to create new opportunities for exploiting old assumptions about women's labor-force participation. The practices discussed above could be used to block the progress that women have made in the labor force over the past ten to fifteen years. Just as women made huge strides in professional and managerial work, those levels of the corporation are being slashed away. Just as women have shattered stereotypes that define "women's work," corporations seem to be building whole new domains of emotionally laden occupations for which women may be seen as prime candidates. And just as women are being taken seriously as full-time workers with deep and meaningful commitments to professional and administrative work, firms are developing part-time and temporary ghettos within these occupational levels and are managing to marginalize even historically elite workers.

Because of the overwhelming presence of women in lower-

18. Marital status will also be important. If a woman is a member of a dual-career couple, her personal flexibility to choose when to work and when not to work will be greater than if she is single and depends on her own income.

level clerical, service, and retail sales jobs (Rothschild 1981), it has long been clear to students of gender relations that women workers have an enduring relationship to the postindustrial economy. The phenomena described above, however, show other ways that women's work and gender inequality will be an integral part of changing authority relations and corporate hierarchies in the restructuring, postindustrial workplace.

The Politics of Restructuring

In theorizing and creating new work arrangements, corporate managers and the postindustrialists must also deal with the general politics of restructuring. Whether and how workers and middle managers resist restructuring will be critical to top management's attempt to gain greater control over the corporation. It appears that more and more corporate employees, managerial and nonmanagerial alike, are sharply critical of short-term strategies for profitability and investment and are challenging top management's prerogative to make decisions that devastate communities, firms, and occupational groups.

Nonmanagerial workers have, in varied circumstances, resisted paying for corporate downsizing with their own efforts (in the form of speedups) and with their own jobs. They have attacked corporate diversification policies that strip productive enterprises of profitability. Because their struggles have had an institutionalized, legal form, located within a formal bargaining framework, such resistance has been far more discernible and "measurable" than managerial resistance.

Union leaders and members, for example, have pressed for legislation to restrict plant closings at the local, state, and national levels (Deitch and Erickson 1987; Lawrence 1987; Staudohar and Brown 1987, part 5). The 1986 steelworkers' strike at U.S. Steel was inspired by distrust of top management's investment and diversification policies (*Businessweek*, 19 May 1986; Hoerr 1988). To halt Safeway Stores' top management from making unilateral decisions about selling off assets and laying off workers, the United Food and Commercial Workers mobilized to gain some degree of veto power in these negotiations (*Businessweek*, 8 September 1986).

In one recent and highly publicized case of opposition to paying the costs of corporate restructuring, the United Airlines contingent of the Airline Pilots Association attempted to buy the airline company from UAL Incorporated, its parent company. This bid was pursued expressly in opposition to UAL's diversification strategies. The pilots argued that top management's policies would jeopardize the airline; the pilots predicted job loss, disruption of business, and a general drain of United Airlines financial resources as top management continued to acquire other businesses (*Wall Street Journal*, 9 April 1987; *Businessweek*, 20 April 1987). They proposed, in return for a controlling interest and ownership by the entire United work force, a leveraged buyout using pension fund money and labor cost reductions.

Similar criticisms guided the recent strike by Eastern Airlines machinists. Machinists and pilots fought company head Frank Lorenzo's notorious agenda to break up the company and sell off assets without regard for the long-term integrity of the airline (*New York Times*, 9 March 1989). Other manufacturing and production unions have bought out plants that top managements were threatening to shut down (Whyte 1987).[19]

My study suggests that managers' resistance to paying the costs of restructuring have been hidden within the firm. I documented some forms of this resistance in American Security Bank and explained how they were shaped by the politics of corporate restructuring. Preliminary evidence from other large corporations suggests similar patterns in the complex in-firm politics of management restructuring.

19. For a cogent criticism of mismanagement from labor's perspective, see the special issue *Labor Research Review* on this topic ("Mismanagement" 1987).

General Motors, a firm that has surfaced occasionally throughout these pages, experienced a major managerial crisis in the face of reorganization processes that cut back both blue- and white-collar workers severely. One report, which framed this crisis as a morale problem, focused on the depression and anger felt by managers who faced the possible disappearance of their own jobs, as well as the pressures and strains of having to "select subordinates as candidates for 'voluntary departure.' " Managers' contradictory position as agents and objects of GM's contraction evoked such a wide reaction that top management identified it as a genuine company problem (*Wall Street Journal*, 26 May 1987b). American Telephone and Telegraph reported a similar "managerial morale crisis." In the wake of its breakup, and extreme cost and personnel cuts, AT & T's middle managers were "deeply disturbed and disillusioned" (*CommunicationsWeek*, 16 February 1987).

These are unsystematic references, to be sure. But although some may persist in calling the subject of this study a "managerial morale crisis," such accounts provide glimpses of profound disturbances in the largest and most powerful corporations in the country. One may reasonably speculate that the real extent to which the in-firm politics of corporate restructuring are blocking and reshaping corporate management directives is much greater than has been revealed.

Similarly little understood are the ways middle management and professional opposition to corporate restructuring agendas can force top management itself to restructure. In other words, top management may have to change its policies when large groups of employees refuse to participate in them; boards of directors can take action to oust those at the top if strategic management fails to gain the consent of key groups in the firm.

In the case of American Security Bank, for example, under pressure from the board of directors, chief executive officer Wedgewood eventually was forced to step down from his position when it became apparent that his policies had failed and that middle managers were not going to manage out massive numbers of "unnecessary" workers. Although it was not the exclusive cause of his departure, middle management refusal added to the impression that the restructuring project in general was failing. United Airlines's parent company similarly jettisoned its corporate head, Richard Ferris, when it became clear that no restructuring program would work without the cooperation of company employees; top management felt that banks would be willing to finance a restructuring plan if the company had the consent of its workers (*New York Times*, 12 June 1987).

Certainly, different groups of workers possess different degrees of organizational capacity and political leverage to resist paying the often severe price of restructuring. One of the most significant differences is between managers and workers who have been targeted for different roles in the new corporate division of labor. While strategic management encourages workers to manage themselves up to self-managers, it encourages middle managers to manage out workers and management itself, goals that appear to be at cross-purposes.

Nevertheless, by articulating and acting on these criticisms, corporate workers, managerial and nonmanagerial alike, resist paying the multiple costs of restructuring. They have taken a critical and oppositional stance to diversification and investment strategies. Perhaps if the agenda to scale down management, embedded at present within change programs that tend to disguise the degradation of management, becomes explicit and more openly coercive, managers' resistance will become much more visibly tied to the resistance of those they manage. Although it would be atypical in view of the history of unionization in the United States, some have suggested that managerial workers might affiliate with traditional blue-collar unions or form white-collar unions (Osterman 1988, p. 81).[20] It is difficult to predict whether work-

20. The *Wall Street Journal* (3 March 1987) recently speculated that white-collar, professional, and managerial employees in Gen-

ers in such disparate positions in the corporate division of labor could collectively embrace an antistrategic management politics, or whether such a politics would have the power to stop rather than simply contain the effects of restructuring (Burawoy 1983). Like the future of the workplace, these political currents remain to be observed and analyzed further. But as Kanter and Mirvis (1989) note, workers at all levels—blue-collar, white-collar, professional, and managerial—have become exceedingly cynical about American corporate management policy, particularly as a result of many of the contradictory processes that have been outlined in this book. Corporate employees distrust the "managerial evangelism" whereby business leaders use "smoke and mirrors schemes" to manipulate workers (Kanter and Mirvis 1989, chap. 6). Workers have also been disillusioned by the failed promises of employment contracts; their loyalties and commitments have eroded as corporations slash and burn away much of the excess work force. In a climate of cynicism, corporate employees may feel compelled to find systematic and organized ways of battling the business mentality that disregards the well-being of those who make business as usual possible.

Between the postindustrial proposals and the realities of American business policies, then, two paths appear to extend from the current economic morass. The paths start at the same point: a consensus about the need for new corporate strategies and about the organizational designs that should in theory improve American competitiveness and industrial relations. But beyond that point the paths diverge. In the current economic era, corporate management needs the commitments of all its employees. It is unclear whether American corporations will try to gain that commitment by following the high-trust, enlightened model of the postindustrialists, however, or whether they will follow more antagonistic, low-

---

eral Motors might consider affiliating with the blue-collar United Auto Workers union after top management essentially froze the salaries of the former group.

trust, hierarchical, short-term cost-cutting policies. Perhaps it is more likely that firms will pursue low-trust hierarchical policies of cutbacks using the rhetoric of high-trust flexible relations, a course of action well illustrated by the case of American Security Bank.[21]

This book has examined the case of one not atypical path that American corporations can follow, as well as the organizational politics created by that choice. Looking at the labor management, product market, and production process strategies adopted by top management in one restructuring corporation, this book analyzed the effect of those strategies on the firm's industrial relations system. American Security Bank's situation illustrates the depth of the difficulty of achieving fundamental corporate change and demonstrates why U.S. top management may be tempted to follow that troubled path for reconfiguring organizational structures and employment relations, rather than the optimistic suggestions of the postindustrial theorists.

If it is to succeed, the postindustrial model may require that American top management relinquish the absolute control it is accustomed to exert over investment and diversification policies; it may also require that firms give too much genuine power to workers. Perhaps more germane, postindustrialism's high-trust premises may be workable only if business leaders are willing to forgo instantaneous high profit margins, to wait out crises, and invest in building a solid, enduring foundation on which to deal with corporate employ-

---

21. In this regard, United Steel Workers' belief that flexibility is mostly rhetoric has been borne out by recent events. USX top management has allegedly renewed its interest in cooperative work relations with labor, devoting significant resources to building worker involvement. At the same time, however, top management espouses this commitment in a low-trust fashion, deliberately trying to avoid working with union leaders or within the terms of the union contract. Furthermore, even as the company pushes workers to be involved in managing, it is violating some terms of the union contract by continuing to subcontract production tasks to nonunion suppliers (*Businessweek*, 26 June 1989).

ees. If we look at the reigning short-term profit outlook and the reassertion of ownership in the 1980s, during which Wall Street gained tremendous influence in determining investment and diversification strategies, we see few signs that American corporations are ready to engage in such a constructive long-term endeavor. At the same time, this study suggests that if corporate managements follow a path that shifts responsibility for corporate upheaval and decline onto its lower-level employees, they may produce high-conflict situations in which managers and workers alike refuse to go along blindly with draconian corporate agendas.

Finally, let us return to the larger question of the future of management. Will "management, as a traditionally conceived, hierarchical function . . . disappear altogether" as one prominent management theorist speculates (Schein 1989, p. 65)? Or will corporate leaders solve their competitive problems through other strategic and organizational means? Whether or not bureaucracies and middle management must be revamped in order to regain corporate competitiveness is a question that is beyond the scope of this study. Certainly such theorists as Zuboff, Hirschhorn, and Hoerr present compelling evidence that the new technologies, combined with current economic exigencies, make it imperative to dislodge exclusive responsibility from the ranks of management and to develop more cooperation between workers and corporate management.

But the lack of research about correlations between the structure of management and profitability, and about other possible internal sources of current economic problems, makes the analysis presented here of the causes and consequences of restructuring all the more important. Corporate top managements have all too willingly scapegoated middle management for alleged problems of hierarchy and rigidity. In the absence of persuasive scholarly evidence to the contrary, they will have full license to continue to cut and degrade management, often at the expense of both managers and workers.

This study proposes a different interpretation of the roots

of the competitive dilemma. It suggests that corporate management strategies ultimately create organizational hierarchies and behavior. What many consider rigid middle-managerial bureaucracies are in fact products of empire building by corporate managers themselves; in a particular economic context those bureaucracies more than fulfilled their purpose. But throughout much of the twentieth century, strategic management at American Security Bank and numerous other corporations developed aggressive profit strategies that were shortsighted in two important senses and led eventually to the demise of bureaucratic management structures. They relied myopically on assumptions of endless growth, and they strove for immediate, maximum short-term returns at the expense of building structure and investing in technologies that would endure in a very different global context. Those strategies have forced corporate top management to make choices about regaining power and profits, and for the most part, they appear to be exercising quick-fix choices that target relatively powerless parties.

By acquitting middle management of ultimate blame for U.S. competitive problems, I do not intend to canonize individual middle managers. To be sure, middle managers may be complacent and may build personal empires at the expense of the larger goals of the corporation (criticisms that have been incorporated into the standard lexicon for scapegoating middle management). I am rather taking a structural perspective on the problem, arguing that we cannot accept at face value that these phenomena explain America's current competitive position. The most important determinant of the failure of the large corporation is top management strategic decision making; the extensive, semi-autonomous structure of middle management was historically a direct by-product of those decisions.

The case of American Security Bank shows that, far from being a major impediment to contemporary restructuring, middle managers in many ways held the social and productive fabric of the corporation together in the face of strategic management's drastic, albeit disguised, objectives. Middle managers carried a different conception of the firm's corporate interest, inspired in part by an explicit criticism of aggressive, shortsighted growth strategies. Because of this criticism, top management lost its credibility for engaging middle managers in the dirty work of restructuring. Middle managers, however, did not dismiss the possibility of overhauling the employee relations framework; instead, they put the brakes on this process, slowing it down, reinterpreting and reworking the new policies both to increase productivity and to maintain the credibility of the firm in the eyes of their employees. From strategic management's perspective, with its insistence on immediate and profitable results, middle managers' actions most certainly were an obstacle; from the perspective of thinking about the future of the American corporation and the prospects for consent to and legitimation of change, middle managers' actions could, in a different strategic context, make possible the cooperation so highly touted by both policy analysts and strategic managers.

Some may wish to say that when it comes to formulating remedies for our economic situation, it matters little who is responsible for the current crisis in the corporation: we should just face the facts and look for new ways of working that will increase productivity and efficiency, even if that means laying off hundreds of thousands of managerial employees and turning remaining workers into controlled managers. Yet there is no reason to think that these policies will be viable in the long run if they are based on inadequate or distorted explanations of how American firms ended up where they are today. This study has attempted to go to the origins of the problem and to relay a sense of the consequences of blindly pursuing corporate employment strategies without regard to the history and power relations of the modern corporation.

Appendix:
Involved Observations in
Training Seminars

I spent approximately seventy-five hours in two week-long management training seminars and observed a total of thirty-seven managers and six trainers. Of the thirty-seven participants, twenty-two were women and fifteen were men; twenty-nine were white and eight were black and other minorities. For the participants in both seminars, the average tenure in the bank was eight years. The seminars I attended were run by small mixed-gender groups (two women and one man in one case, two men and one woman in the other); in addition, a stream of future trainers, as well as those coordinating the seminars, flowed through each seminar with little or no warning and sat in the back of the room as observers.

I cross-checked my observations with twelve managers from the seminars with whom I conducted follow-up interviews; I interviewed other managers (whom I did not observe) about their seminar experiences. Managers in the management development division gave me permission to observe and interview seminar participants. The trainers and the participants at the seminars I attended knew that I was a sociologist from the University of California, studying the response of middle managers to corporate change. My role was a peculiar one, insofar as I believe that my presence was somewhat a challenge to the trainers. They prided themselves on a social-scientific approach to working with managers and thus took my role and my work very seriously.

For this reason, they occasionally, on and off during the

seminars, attempted to manage my perception of the seminar proceedings by talking with me about events that were "objectively true" and those that were merely "subjective opinions." In both seminars, the trainers seated me between them at the trainers' table. This position—I was wedged in between them—gave them many opportunities to peer over my shoulder to examine my notes, which they did quite frequently. When one particularly contentious participant was going on about the problems with top management, one of the trainers went to great lengths to let me know that this person was unusually prickly and that she had rarely seen any manager react in the fashion he did. Because I had observed these dynamics before, and because in interviews other managers had described similar controversies in seminars they attended, her comment seemed to arise from some sense of alarm that an outsider would draw the conclusion that the management seminars were something other than consensual and harmonious. That same trainer also went to great lengths to assure me that some interactions I had recorded reflected only one person's opinion about the corporation.

Despite the fact that I was not a participant in the fashion typical of the participant observer (Becker 1970) (that is, I was not filling the shoes of the participant working as a manager, and I was not the direct target of the trainers' resocialization efforts), I was nevertheless an involved observer, a participant in a different and important way. Much as for the "observer as participant" (Gold 1970), involved observation allowed me to interact with trainers and participants and to assess, from their diverse perspectives, the progress and obstacles of the seminars.

During the numerous breaks taken throughout the seminar, various participants approached me, seeking out my opinion about what I had observed and sharing with me the "deep" feelings they felt they could not express in the context of the seminar group. As an involved observer, I frequently felt like a partial participant.

Involved participation created an occasional dilemma for

me. After one prolonged and contentious debate between seminar trainers and participants, one of the trainers asked whether I would mind giving her a copy of my notes, which contained a near-verbatim record of the exchange. Because she was very confused about the participants' anger, and because she was unwilling to believe that these managers were unjustified in their anger, she felt that the trainers could benefit from going over the interaction at a later time. I was loath to lend her my notes as it was conceivable that the trainers might retaliate against certain seminar participants. Fortunately, I was able to refuse politely on the grounds that I was obligated to preserve confidentiality for all the people I was observing, trainers and seminar participants alike, an explanation she accepted.

I recorded by hand all seminar interactions; along with my notes I maintained an informal coding system that allowed me to note not only spoken passages but voice inflections, silences (where trainers failed to respond to specific issues raised by participants), unanticipated activities (trainers pacing about, calling unscheduled breaks as a response to tense moments), and particular types of interactions (contentious, consensual, and the like). After each seminar I wrote extensive notes on my observations.

The material in Chapter 3 is presented not sequentially but topically. Because the curriculum was the same in both seminars, and because the seminar dynamics were strikingly similar (both in the way they were taught and in managers' responses), I have combined the data from the two seminars and organized them according to significant themes. Although there were other important topics (for example, the problems in shifting to the pay-for-performance or merit plan), I use the discussion of minimum job requirements and structural changes because they clearly illuminate middle managers' concerns and trainers' objectives and discourse.

Glossary

Bell Curve. A normal distribution of employee performance that supposedly characterized every manager's unit. Managers were told that if they ranked all their employees along a scale of one to four, each group would "naturally" fall along a normal curve, with 15 percent on the bottom, 15 percent on top, and 70 percent in between. To press home their point visually that middle managers had historically been too complacent in the way they managed, the trainers in the seminars argued that the peak of the existing curve arched over point number one. The curve was supposed to peak between two and three, and one of the trainers' objectives was to push managers to "normalize" their curves by downranking their employees. Another objective was to get managers to manage out those employees who fell on the bottom 15 percent of the curve.

Minimum Job Requirements. The baseline job description for any given position. MJRs could be different for jobs that were roughly equivalent, depending on the sector in which the job was located. For example, data-entry work in the credit card center might have different MJRs from data-entry work in the check-processing division. Managers in diverse units were often responsible for determining the MJRs.

Nonnegotiable Changes. Trainers' terminology for any structural change passed down from the higher echelons of the firm that neither managers nor nonmanagerial employees could control. Such changes included branch or other unit closure, the removal of functions from work sites (such as the removal of mass-market lending activities from branches), or the introduction of new computerized technology.

Performance Planning, Coaching, and Evaluation (PPCE). An evaluation form introduced in 1983 as part of the middle management overhaul. The PPCE form consisted of three or four parts, depending on whether the individual being evaluated was a nonmanagerial employee (three pages) or a manager (four pages). As the words "performance planning," "coaching," and "evaluation" suggest, the PPCE allowed for documentation of the following issues: the performance objectives for the employee; how achievement of those objectives would be measured; a written evaluation of the results (whether the individual met, fully met, or far exceeded objectives); a performance summary, in which both manager and employee rated and commented on the employee's work; and the coaching sessions, in which the manager informed the employee of his or her progress three times within the year following the written report.

Both manager and employee had to agree on the performance objectives and the basis for measuring performance. Strategic management insisted, in its "open statements" to employees in the bank newspaper, that it was this process of "mutual" discussion of job performance that made the PPCE so important, rather than the actual form itself. Designed to draw in both the manager and the employee, the PPCE provided a mechanism for heightened involvement and participation in setting and achieving goals. It was a highly individualizing mechanism: the manager could set objectives that varied from individual to individual; negotiations about the degree to which employees achieved their objectives occurred in a similarly individualized way. By requiring documentation of four evaluation sessions per year, the PPCE institutionalized negotiation sessions between the manager and the employee over what the employee was to accomplish. (Both signed and dated the agreement when it was first written and again at year's end, at which time a new form was filled out. The manager's manager also had to approve the document at the end of the year, thus tying managers together in a vertical line of accountability.)

Evaluation forms for managers contained an additional "Management Supplement," which specified, for the first time in the bank's history, how managers would be evaluated on "managing people," emphasized strongly in the management seminars. (In fact, strategic management, in the bank's management newsletter, dubbed the PPCE the "People Maximizer" because it would "enable employees to maximize their contribution to the bank.")

These specifications included how well a manager had staffed his or her unit; whether or not a manager was appropriately recognizing and rewarding positive achievement; how well a manager communicated; how well the manager conducted the PPCE process with employees; whether the manager was a "good leader"; and whether the manager understood and implemented the principles and goals of affirmative action. One-third of a manager's evaluation was to be based on how well he or she managed people. The PPCE formalized the managerial task by providing specific criteria while simultaneously organizing new areas of responsibility and effort.

Raising the Bar. Raising the baseline productivity standards, the minimum job requirements, for any given position.

Situational Leadership. A theory of worker psychology and the way managers should address different psychological orientations. Based on the work of organizational behaviorists (Hershey and Blanchard 1977), the theory of situational leadership contained a detailed analysis of how managers should approach each and every one of their employees. According to this framework each employee required different degrees and types of managerial intervention, the extent of which was to be deciphered by a combination of managerial intuition and "scientific" management tools. It was as important for a manager to know when to leave an employee alone as it was to know who must be closely supervised. The more "mature" an employee, in terms of being willing and able to accomplish tasks, the less a manager needed to tell that person what to do, since presumably the employee possessed adequate internal resources and incentives for achieving. At the other end of the spectrum, "immature" employees required constant guidance and monitoring because, for whatever reason, they were incapable of directing their efforts toward the objectives of their unit.

To help decipher individual employees' proclivities, middle managers and supervisors were given a diagram of a personality curve that they were to use to interpret various work situations and employees. The diagram, however, was never to be seen as more than a tool to aid the real managerial weapon, the "Big J," a manager's own personal judgment. Thus situational leadership called for managers to dip into the reservoir of their instinctual managerial authority and take an active, intensified role in the work and psychological orientation of all employees in the bank.

Stretch Objectives. Productivity levels set over and above minimum job requirements. Employees were pushed to "stretch" to achieve these objectives, which could include quantitative increases in output (increasing numbers of sales, completion of a project by a given date, decreasing the number of customer complaints) and qualitative changes (exhibiting positive attitudes toward change, showing "team spirit," and so forth). Managers were told, in the training seminars, that they should refer to the following factors to justify new, higher objectives to their employees: the employee's personal capacity for change and improvement, quotas the manager herself or himself must fulfill, technological conditions, and the peculiarities of the geographical region.

Bibliography

Adler, Paul. 1986. "New Technologies, New Skills." *California Management Review* 29 (1): 9–28.

Argyris, Chris. 1955. "Organizational Leadership and Participative Management." *Journal of Business* 28 (1): 1–7.

Athos, Anthony, and Richard Pascale. 1981. *The Art of Japanese Management: Applications for American Executives.* New York: Simon & Schuster.

Baran, Barbara, and Suzanne Teegarden. 1987. "Women's Labor in the Office of the Future: A Case Study of the Insurance Industry." Pp. 201–224 in Lourdres Beneria and Catherine Stimpson, eds. *Women, Households and the Economy.* New Brunswick, N. J.: Rutgers University Press.

Baron, James, and William Bielby. 1980. "Bringing the Firms Back In: Stratification, Segmentation, and the Organization of Work." *American Sociological Review* 45 (5): 737–765.

Becker, Howard. 1970. "Problems in Inference and Proof in Participant Observation." Pp. 25–38 in *Sociological Work: Method and Substance.* Chicago: Aldine Publishing.

Beer, Michael, and Bert Spector. 1985. "Corporatewide Transformations in Human Resource Management." Pp. 219–253 in Richard Walton and Paul Lawrence, eds. *Human Resources Management: Trends and Challenges.* Boston: Harvard Business School Press.

Bell, Daniel. 1973. *The Coming of Post-Industrial Society.* New York: Basic Books.

Bendix, Reinhard. 1956. *Work and Authority in Industry: Ideologies of Management in the Course of Industrialization.* Berkeley and Los Angeles: University of California Press.

Berg, Ivar, Marcia Freedman, and Michael Freeman. 1978. *Managers and Work Reform: A Limited Engagement.* New York: Free Press.

Berle, Adolph, and Gardiner Means. 1968. *The Modern Corporation and Private Property.* New York: Harcourt, Brace & World.

Berman, Melissa, ed. 1986. *Corporate Culture and Change.* Report from the Conference Board. Report No. 888.

Biggart, Nicole. 1983. "Rationality, Meaning, and Self-Management: Success Manuals, 1950–1980." *Social Problems* 30 (3): 298–311.

Blau, Peter. 1955. *The Dynamics of Bureaucracy.* Chicago: University of Chicago Press.

Blau, Peter, and Richard Schoenherr. 1971. *The Structure of Organizations.* New York: Basic Books.

Block, Fred. 1986. "Productivity as a Social Problem: The Uses and Misuses of Social Indicators." *American Sociological Review* 51 (1): 767–780.

Bluestone, Barry, and Bennett Harrison. 1982. *The Deindustrialization of America.* New York: Basic Books.

Blum, Linda, and Vicki Smith. 1988. "Women's Mobility in the Corporation: A Critique of the Politics of Optimism." *Signs: Journal of Women in Culture and Society* 13 (3): 528–545.

Blumberg, Paul. 1975. "Alienation and Participation." Pp. 324–338 in Jaroslav Vanek, ed. *Self-Management: Economic Liberation of Man.* Harmondsworth: Penguin Books.

Bolwijn, P. T., and T. Kumpe. 1986. "Toward the Factory of the Future." *McKinsey Quarterly,* Spring, pp. 40–49.

Bowles, Samuel, David Gordon, and Thomas Weisskopf. 1984. *Beyond the Wasteland: A Democratic Alternative to Economic Decline.* Garden City, New Jersey: Anchor Press/ Doubleday.

Bradley, Keith, and Stephen Hill. 1987. "Quality Circles and Managerial Interests." *Industrial Relations* 26 (1): 68–82.

Brand, Horst, and John Duke. 1982. "Productivity in Commercial Banking: Computers Spur the Advance." *Monthly Labor Review* 105 (12): 19–27.

Brandt, Steven. 1986. *Entrepreneurs in Established Companies: Managing Toward the Year 2000*. New York: New American Library.

Braverman, Harry. 1974. *Labor and Monopoly Capital: The Degradation of Labor in the Twentieth Century*. New York: Monthly Review Press.

Brewer, E., and J. W. C. Tomlinson. 1964. "The Manager's Working Day." *Journal of Industrial Economics* 12 (3): 191–197.

Bunker, Barbara, and Howard Williams. 1986. "Managing Organizational Decline." *Personnel* 63 (6): 31–40.

Burawoy, Michael. 1979. *Manufacturing Consent: Changes in the Labor Process under Monopoly Capitalism*. Chicago: University of Chicago Press.

———. 1983. "Between the Labor Process and the State: The Changing Face of Factory Regimes Under Advanced Capitalism." *American Sociological Review* 48 (5): 587–605.

Burawoy, Michael, and János Lukács. 1989. "What is Socialist about Socialist Production? Autonomy and Control in a Hungarian Steel Mill." Pp. 295–316 in Stephen Wood, ed. *The Transformation of Work? Skill, Flexibility and the Labour Process*. London: Unwin Hyman.

Bureau of National Affairs. 1986. *The Changing Workplace: New Directions in Staffing and Scheduling*. Bureau of National Affairs. 1231 25th St., N.W. Room N-215. Washington, D.C.

Burnham, James. 1941. *The Managerial Revolution*. New York: John Day Co.

Businessweek. 20 December 1982. "A Flood of Pinkslips for Middle Management." Pp. 20–21.

———. 25 April 1983a. "A New Era for Management." Pp. 50–53.

———. 25 April 1983b. "The Shrinking of Middle Management." Pp. 54–61.

———. 14 May 1984. "Changing a Corporate Culture." Pp. 130–138.

———. 21 January 1985. "The New Corporate Elite." Pp. 62–81.

———. 7 April 1986. "Roger Smith's Campaign to Change the GM Culture." Pp. 84–85.

———. 19 May 1986. "Bad Blood at Big Steel Could Lead to a Costly Strike." Pp. 82–84.

———. 7 July 1986. "IBM's Fancy Footwork to Sidestep Layoffs." Pp. 54–55.

———. 4 August 1986. "The End of Corporate Loyalty?" Pp. 42–49.

———. 8 September 1986. "A Union's Novel Attempt at Shaping a Buyout." P. 31.

———. 27 October 1986. "What Ails Corporate America—And What Should Be Done." P. 101.

———. 20 April 1987. "UAL's Pilots May Put the Airline into Play." P. 25.

———. 12 September 1988. "Caught in the Middle: Six Managers Speak Out on Corporate Life." Pp. 80–88.

———. 20 March 1989. "The Mommy Track." Pp. 126–134.

———. 26 June 1989. "Suddenly, USX Is Playing Mr. Nice Guy." Pp. 151–152.

———. 10 July 1989. "The Payoff from Teamwork." Pp. 56–62.

Cameron, Kim, R. Sutton, and D. Whetton. 1988. "Introduction: Issues in Organizational Decline." Pp. 3–19 in *Readings in Organizational Decline.* Cambridge, Mass.: Ballinger Publishing Co.

Cameron, Kim, and Raymond Zammuto. 1988. "Matching Managerial Strategies to Conditions of Decline." Pp. 117–128 in K. Cameron, R. Sutton, and D. Whetton, eds. *Readings in Organizational Decline.* Cambridge, Mass.: Ballinger Publishing Co.

Cameron, Kim, M. Kim, and D. Whetton. 1987. "Organizational Effects of Decline and Turbulence." *Administrative Science Quarterly* 32 (2): 222–240.

Capelli, Peter, and Robert McKersie. 1987. "Management Strategy and the Redesign of Workrules." *Journal of Management Studies* 24 (5): 440–462.

Carey, Max, and Kim Hazelbaker. 1986. "Employment Growth in the Temporary Help Industry." *Monthly Labor Review* 109 (4): 37–44.

Chandler, Alfred. 1962. *Strategy and Structure: Chapters in the History of the Industrial Enterprise*. Cambridge, Mass.: MIT Press.

———. 1977. *The Visible Hand: The Managerial Revolution in American Business*. Cambridge, Mass.: Harvard University Press, Belknap Press.

Child, John. 1977. *Organization: A Guide to Problems and Practice*. London: Harper & Row.

Clawson, Dan. 1980. *Bureaucracy and the Labor Process: The Transformation of U.S. Industry, 1860–1920*. New York: Monthly Review Press.

Clegg, Stewart. 1981. "Organization and Control." *Administrative Science Quarterly* 26 (4): 545–562.

Clegg, Stewart, and David Dunkerly. 1980. *Organization, Class and Control*. London: Routledge & Kegan Paul.

Cohen, Stephen, and John Zysman. 1987. *Manufacturing Matters: The Myth of the Post-Industrial Economy*. New York: Basic Books.

Collins, Sharon. 1989. "The Marginalization of Black Executives." *Social Problems* 36 (4): 317–331.

CommunicationsWeek. 16 February 1987. "AT & T Psychologist Documents Companywide Morale Crisis." Pp. 1, 12.

Corrigan, Richard, and Rochelle Stanfield. 1984. "Casualties of Change." *National Journal* 11 (February): 252–264.

Crozier, Michel. 1964. *The Bureaucratic Phenomenon*. Chicago: University of Chicago Press.

Dahrendorf, Ralph. 1959. *Class and Class Conflict in Industrial Society*. Stanford, Calif.: Stanford University Press.

Dalton, Melville. 1959. *Men Who Manage*. New York: John Wiley & Sons.

Darby, Michael. 1984. "The U.S. Productivity Slowdown: A Case of Statistical Myopia." *American Economic Review* 74 (3): 301–322.

Dawson, P., and I. McLoughlin. 1986. "Computer Technology and the Redefinition of Supervision: A Study of the Effects of Computerization on Railway Freight Supervisors." *Journal of Management Studies* 23 (1): 116–132.

Deitch, Cynthia, and Robert Erickson. 1987. " 'Save Dorothy': A Political Response to Structural Change in the Steel Industry." Pp. 241–279 in R. Lee, ed. *Redundancy, Layoffs and Plant Closures*. London: Croom Helm.

Delehanty, George. 1968. *Nonproduction Workers in U.S. Manufacturing*. Amsterdam: North-Holland Publishing Co.

Dickson, John. 1981. "Participation as a Means of Organizational Control." *Journal of Management Studies* 18 (2): 159–176.

Drago, Robert. 1988. "Quality Circle Survival: An Exploratory Analysis." *Industrial Relations* 27 (3): 336–351.

Dun's Business Month. July 1985. "The No Lay-off Payoff." Pp. 64–66.

Edwards, Richard. 1979. *Contested Terrain: The Transformation of the Workplace in the Twentieth Century*. New York: Basic Books.

Fallows, James. 1985. "America's Changing Economic Landscape." *The Atlantic Monthly*, March, pp. 47–68.

Feldman, Steven. 1986. "Management in Context: An Essay on the Relevance of Culture to the Understanding of Organizational Change." *Journal of Management Studies* 23 (6): 587–607.

Ferris, Gerald, Deborah Schellenberg, and Raymond Zammuto. 1984. "Human Resource Management Strategies in Declining Industries." *Human Resource Management* 23 (4): 381–394.

Fischer, Frank, and Carmen Sirianni, eds. 1984. *Critical Stud-*

ies in Organization and Bureaucracy. Philadelphia: Temple University Press.

Flaim, Paul, and Ellen Sehgal. 1987. "Reemployment and Earnings." Pp. 101–130 in Paul Staudohar and Holly Brown, eds. *Deindustrialization and Plant Closure.* Lexington, Mass.: D. C. Heath, Lexington Books. Originally published as "Displaced Workers of 1979–83: How Well Have They Fared?" *Monthly Labor Review* 108 (6): 3–16.

Fortune. 20 September 1982. "Hard Times Catch up with Executives." Pp. 50–54.

———. 6 February 1984. "The Recovery Skips Middle Managers." Pp. 112–120.

———. 28 October 1985a. "Management Layoffs Won't Quit." Pp. 46–49.

———. 28 October 1985b. "Managers Without a Company." Pp. 51–56.

———. 10 November 1986. "GM is Tougher Than You Think." Pp. 56–64.

———. 2 February 1987. "The Economy of the 1990s: How Managers Will Manage." Pp. 47–50.

———. 2 March 1987. "Pushed out at 45: Now What?" Pp. 26–30.

Freedman, Audrey. 1988. "How the 1980s Changed Industrial Relations." *Monthly Labor Review* 111 (5): 35–38.

Freeman, Richard, and James Medoff. 1984. *What Do Unions Do?* New York: Basic Books.

Friedman, Andrew. 1977. *Industry and Labour.* London: Macmillan.

Fulmer, Robert. 1986. "Educating Managers for the Future." *Personnel* 63 (2): 70–73.

Gardner, Burleigh, and William F. Whyte. 1945. "The Man in the Middle: Position and Problems of the Foreman." *Applied Anthropology* 4 (2): 1–28.

Gilmore, Thomas, and Larry Hirschhorn. 1983. "Management Challenges Under Conditions of Retrenchment." *Human Resource Management* 22 (4): 341–357.

Ginzberg, Eli, and George Vojta. 1985. *Beyond Human Scale.* New York: Basic Books.

Gold, Raymond. 1970. "Roles in Sociological Field Observations." Pp. 370–380 in Norman Denzin, ed. *Sociological Methods: A Sourcebook.* Chicago: Aldine Publishing.

Gordon, Jack. 1986a. "*Training* Magazine's Industry Report 1986." *Training: Magazine of Human Resources Development* 23 (10): 26–28.

———. 1986b. "Where the Training Goes." *Training: Magazine of Human Resources Development* 23 (10): 49–68.

Gough, Jamie. 1986. "Industrial Policy and Socialist Strategy: Restructuring and the Unity of the Working Class." *Capital and Class* 29 (Summer): 58–81.

Gouldner, Alvin. 1954. *Patterns of Industrial Bureaucracy.* New York: Free Press.

Greenbaum, Joan. 1979. *In the Name of Efficiency: Management Theory and Shopfloor Practice in Data-Processing Work.* Philadelphia: Temple University Press.

Greenhalgh, L., R. McKersie, and R. Gilkey. 1986. "Rebalancing the Workforce at IBM: A Case Study of Redeployment and Revitalization." *Organizational Dynamics* 14 (4): 30–47.

Grenier, Guillermo. 1988. *Inhuman Relations: Anti-Unionism in American Industry.* Philadelphia: Temple University Press.

Hales, Colin. 1986. "What Do Managers Do? A Critical Review of the Evidence." *Journal of Management Studies* 23 (1): 88–115.

Hall, Douglas, and Lynn Isabella. 1985. "Downward Movement and Career Development." *Organizational Dynamics* 14 (1): 5–23.

Halloran, Keith D. 1985. "The Impact of Merger and Acquisition Programs on Corporate Identity." *Mergers and Acquisitions* 20 (1): 60–66.

Hammer, Tove, and Robert Stern. 1986. "A Yo-Yo Model of Cooperation: Union Participation in Management at the Rath Packing Company." *Industrial and Labor Relations Review* 39 (3): 337–349.

Hardy, Cynthia, and Andrew Pettigrew. 1985. "The Use of Power in Managerial Strategies for Change." Pp. 11–45 in Richard Rosenbloom, ed. *Research on Technological Innovation, Management and Policy* 2. Greenwich, Conn.: JAI Press.

Harrigan, Kathryn. 1988. *Managing Maturing Businesses: Restructuring Declining Industries and Revitalizing Troubled Operations*. Lexington, Mass.: Lexington Books.

Hartman, Frank, and Robert Hill. 1983. "New Life for Ailing Big Firms by Cutting Them Down to Size." *Management Review* 72 (6): 17–22.

Hayes, Robert, and William Abernathy. 1980. "Managing Our Way to Economic Decline." *Harvard Business Review* 58 (4): 67–77.

Helfgott, Roy. 1988. *Computerized Manufacturing and Human Resources*. Lexington, Mass.: D. C. Heath, Lexington Books.

Henderson, Jeffrey, and Manuel Castells, eds. 1987. *Global Restructuring and Territorial Development*. London: Sage Publications.

Hershey, Paul, and Kenneth Blanchard. 1977. *Management of Organizational Behavior: Utilizing Human Resources*. Englewood Cliffs, N.J.: Prentice-Hall.

Hickey, John. 1987. "GE: Self-Directed Work Teams Make Less Supervision Better." *Work in America*, February, pp. 1–2.

Hirsch, Paul. 1975. "Organization Analysis and Industrial Sociology." *American Sociologist* 10 (1): 3–12.

Hirschhorn, Larry. 1984. *Beyond Mechanization*. Cambridge, Mass.: MIT Press.

———. 1988. "The Post-Industrial Economy: Labor, Skills and the New Mode of Production." *Service Industries*, January.

Hochschild, Arlie. 1983. *The Managed Heart*. Berkeley and Los Angeles: University of California Press.

Hodgetts, Jane, Paul Lawrence, and Leonard Schlesinger. 1985. "Tiner Trucking Industry: From Control to Commitment." *Human Resource Management* 24 (1): 25–50.

Hoerr, John. 1988. *And the Wolf Finally Came: The Decline of the American Steel Industry.* Pittsburgh: University of Pittsburgh Press.

Holland, Max. 1989. *When the Machine Finally Stopped: A Cautionary Tale from Industrial America.* Boston: Harvard Business School Press.

Horne, J. H., and Tom Lupton. 1965. "The Work Activities of 'Middle Managers'—An Exploratory Study." *Journal of Management Studies* 2 (1): 14–33.

Horowitz, Robert. 1986. "Understanding Deregulation." *Theory and Society* 15 (1–2): 139–174.

Howard, Robert. 1985. *Brave New Workplace.* New York: Viking Books.

Jacoby, Sanford. 1984. "The Development of Internal Labor Markets in American Manufacturing Firms." Pp. 23–69 in Paul Osterman, ed. *Internal Labor Markets.* Cambridge, Mass.: MIT Press.

———. 1985. *Employing Bureaucracy: Managers, Unions, and the Transformation of Work in American Industry, 1900–1945.* New York: Columbia University Press.

Jaikumar, Ramchandran. 1986. "Post-Industrial Manufacturing." *Harvard Business Review* 64 (6): 69–76.

John, D. Geoffrey. 1987. "Staffing with Temporary Help." *Personnel Administrator* 32 (1): 96–99.

Judson, Arnold. 1982. "The Awkward Truth About Productivity." *Harvard Business Review* 60 (5): 93–97.

Juravich, Tom. 1985. *Chaos on the Shop Floor: A Worker's View of Quality, Productivity, and Management.* Philadelphia: Temple University Press.

Kanter, Donald, and Philip Mirvis. 1989. *The Cynical Americans: Living and Working in an Age of Discontent and Disillusion.* San Francisco: Jossey-Bass.

Kanter, Rosabeth Moss. 1983. *The Changemasters.* New York: Simon & Schuster.

———. 1986. "The Reshaping of Middle Management." *Management Review* 75 (1): 19–20.

———. 1987. "The Attack on Pay." *Harvard Business Review* 65 (2): 60–67.

Kenney, Martin, and Richard Florida. 1988. "Beyond Mass Production: Production and the Labor Process in Japan." *Politics and Society* 16 (1): 121–158.

Kerr, Clark. 1964. *Industrialism and Industrial Man.* New York: Oxford University Press.

Kimberley, John, and Robert Quinn. 1984. *Managing Organizational Transitions.* Homewood, Ill.: Richard D. Irwin.

Kochan, Thomas, and Peter Capelli. 1984. "The Transformation of the Industrial Relations and Personnel Function." Pp. 133–161 in Paul Osterman, ed. *Internal Labor Markets.* Cambridge, Mass.: MIT Press.

Kochan, Thomas, Harry Katz, and Robert McKersie. 1986. *The Transformation of American Industrial Relations.* New York: Basic Books.

Kotter, John. 1982. "What Effective General Managers Really Do." *Harvard Business Review* 60 (6): 156–167.

Kraft, Philip. 1977. *Programmers and Managers: The Routinization of Computer Programming in the United States.* New York: Springer-Verlag.

Krantz, James. 1988. "Group Process Under Conditions of Organizational Decline." Pp. 265–278 in K. Cameron, R. Sutton, and D. Whetton, eds. *Readings in Organizational Decline.* Cambridge, Mass.: Ballinger Publishing Co.

Kruisinga, H. J. 1954. *The Balance Between Centralization and Decentralization in Managerial Control.* Leiden: H. E. Stenfert Kroese.

Lawler, E., and S. Mohrman. 1985. "Quality Circles After the Fad." *Harvard Business Review* 85 (1): 65–71.

Lawrence, Anne. 1987. "Union Responses to Plant Closure." Pp. 201–215 in Paul Staudohar and Holly Brown, eds. *Deindustrialization and Plant Closure.* Lexington, Mass.: D. C. Heath, Lexington Books.

Lawrence, Paul. 1985. "The History of Human Resource Management in American Industry." Pp. 15–34 in Richard Walton and Paul Lawrence, eds. *Human Resources Management: Trends and Challenges.* Boston: Harvard Business School.

LeGrande, Linda. 1983. *Economic Growth and Changing Labor Markets: Those Left Behind, Dislocated Workers*. Library of Congress, Congressional Research Service. Report no. 83-220E.

Levine, Hermine. 1986. "The Squeeze on Middle Management." *Personnel* 63 (1): 62–69.

Liker, Jeffrey, David Roitman, and Ethel Roskies. 1987. "Changing Everything All at Once: Work Life and Technological Change." *Sloan Management Review* 28 (4): 29–47.

Litterer, Joseph. 1963. "Systematic Management: Design for Organizational Recoupling in American Manufacturing Firms." *Business History Review* 37 (4): 369–391.

Lupton, Tom. 1963. *On the Shop Floor*. Oxford: Pergamon Press.

McClellan, Hassell. 1981. *Managing One-Bank Holding Companies*. New York: Praeger Publishers.

McGregor, Douglas. 1960. *The Human Side of the Enterprise*. New York: McGraw-Hill Book Co.

Mangum, G., D. Mayall, and K. Nelson. 1985. "The Temporary Help Industry: A Response to the Dual Internal Labor Market." *Industrial and Labor Relations Review* 38 (4): 599–611.

Manz, Charles, and Henry Sims. 1987. "Leading Workers to Lead Themselves: The External Leadership of Self-Managing Work Teams." *Administrative Science Quarterly* 32 (1): 106–129.

March, James, and Herbert Simon. 1958. *Organizations*. New York: John Wiley & Sons.

Margolis, Diane R. 1979. *The Managers: Corporate Life in America*. New York: William Morris.

Martin, Thomas. 1988. "Building a Quality Culture at Westinghouse." Pp. 451–469 in Ralph Kilman and Teresa Covin, eds. *Corporate Transformation: Revitalizing Organizations for a Competitive World*. San Francisco: Jossey-Bass.

Melman, Seymour. 1951. "The Rise of Administrative Overhead in the Manufacturing Industries of the U.S., 1899–1947." *Oxford Economic Papers* 3 (1): 62–112.

——. 1983. *Profits Without Production*. New York: Alfred Knopf.

Miller, Richard. 1985. *Banker's Almanac*. Boston: Banker's Publishing Co.

Mills, C. Wright. 1951. *White Collar*. London: Oxford University Press.

Mintzberg, Henry. 1975. "The Manager's Job: Folklore and Fact." *Harvard Business Review* 53 (4): 49–61.

——. 1979. *The Structuring of Organizations*. Englewood Cliffs, N. J.: Prentice-Hall.

"Mismanagement." 1987. *Labor Research Review* 6 (1). Special issue.

Monsen, R. Joseph, and Borje Saxberg. 1977. "When Workers Won't Work and Managers Won't Manage." *Management Review* 66 (8): 26–28, 37–39.

Munro, David. 1985. "Programs and Prospects for Economic Recovery: A Business Perspective." Pp. 194–201 in Betty Lall, ed. *Economic Dislocation and Job Loss*. Ithaca, N.Y.: Cornell University, School of Industrial and Labor Relations.

Naisbett, John. 1982. *Megatrends*. New York: Warner Books.

Nelson, Daniel. 1975. *Managers and Workers: Origins of the New Factory System in the United States, 1880–1920*. Madison: University of Wisconsin Press.

New York Times. 23 June 1982. "The White Collar Pay Freeze." Sec. 4, p. 1.

——. 17 October 1982a. "Merger Mania Adds to Executive Woes." Sec. 12, p. 10.

——. 17 October 1982b. "Middle Managers Are Getting Squeezed Out." Sec. 12, p. 10.

——. 15 December 1982. "Discontent of Middle Managers." Sec. 4, p. 17.

——. 8 November 1986. "Treasury Official Assails 'Inefficient' Big Business." Pp. 1, 28.

——. 4 January 1987. "The Ax Falls on Equal Opportunity." Sec. 3, pp. 1, 27.

————. 22 March 1987. "Managerial Class Gets Roughed Up." Sec. 12, pp. 11–13.

————. 17 April 1987. "Gurus Hired to Motivate Workers Are Raising Fears of 'Mind Control.' " Sec. 1, p. 10.

————. 12 June 1987. "Allegis Hopes to Recruit a Top Labor Negotiator." Sec. 4, pp. 1, 4.

————. 17 August 1987. "Top Tiers Still Elude Corporate Women." Sec. 2, p. 4.

————. 24 January 1988. "Why Being Fired Is Losing Its Taint." Sec. 3, pp. 1, 11.

————. 9 March 1989. "Rare Labor Unity." Sec. 2, p. 15.

Nichols, Theo. 1980. "Management, Ideology and Practice." Pp. 292–302 in Geoff Esland and Graeme Salaman, eds. *The Politics of Work and Occupations*. Toronto: University of Toronto Press.

Nichols, Theo, and Huw Beynon. 1977. *Living with Capitalism: Class Relations and the Modern Factory*. London: Routledge & Kegan Paul.

"1988 Profile." 1989. *Mergers and Acquisitions* 23 (6): 53.

Oaklander, Harold. 1982. "U.S. Policies Toward Redundant Workers." Pp. 187–214 in Edward Yemin, ed. *Workforce Reductions in Undertakings: Policies and Measures for the Protection of Redundant Workers in Seven Industrialized Market Economy Countries*. Geneva: International Labour Office.

"Organizational Culture." 1983. *Administrative Science Quarterly* 28 (3). Special issue.

"Organizational Culture." 1983. *Organizational Dynamics* 12 (2). Special issue.

"Organizational Culture and Control." 1986. *Journal of Management Studies* 23 (3). Special issue.

Osterman, Paul. 1988. *Employment Futures: Reorganization, Dislocation, and Public Policy*. New York: Oxford University Press.

Ouchi, William. 1981. *Theory Z: How American Business Can Meet the American Challenge*. Reading, Mass.: Addison-Wesley Publishing Co.

Ouchi, William, and Alan Wilkins. 1985. "Organizational Cultures." *Annual Review of Sociology* 11: 457–483.

Parker, Mike, and Jane Slaughter. 1988. *Choosing Sides: Unions and the Team Concept.* Boston: South End Press.

Pascale, Richard. 1984. "Fitting New Employees into the Company Culture." *Fortune,* 28 May, pp. 28–42.

Patten, Thomas. 1968. *The Foreman: Forgotten Man of Industry.* New York: American Management Association.

Perlo, Victor. 1982. "The False Claim of Declining Productivity and Its Political Use." *Science and Society* 46 (3): 284–327.

Perrow, Charles. 1986. *Complex Organizations: A Critical Essay.* 3d ed. New York: Random House.

Perry, Lee Tom. 1986. "Least-Cost Alternatives to Layoffs in Declining Industries." *Organizational Dynamics* 14 (4): 48–61.

Peters, Tom. 1985. "Why Smaller Staffs Do Better." *New York Times,* 21 April, sec. 3, pp. 1, 14–15.

Peters, Tom, and Robert Waterman. 1984. *In Search of Excellence: Lessons from America's Best-Run Companies.* New York: Warner Books.

Pfeffer, Jeffrey, and James Baron. 1988. "Taking the Workers Back In: Recent Trends in the Structuring of Employment." Pp. 257–303 in Barry Staw and L. L. Cummings, eds. *Research in Organizational Behavior* 10. Greenwich, Conn.: JAI Press.

Piore, Michael, and Charles Sabel. 1984. *The Second Industrial Divide: Possibilities for Prosperity.* New York: Basic Books.

Prechel, Harland. 1986. *Capital Accumulation and Corporate Rationality: Organizational Change in an American Steel Corporation.* Ph. D. dissertation, University of Kansas.

Raelin, Joseph. 1985. "The Basis for the Professional's Resistance to Managerial Control." *Human Resource Management* 24 (2): 147–175.

Ravenscroft, David, and F. M. Scherer. 1987. *Mergers, Sell-offs and Economic Efficiency.* Washington, D.C.: Brookings Institution.

Ray, Carol Axtell. 1986. "Corporate Culture: The Last Frontier of Control." *Journal of Management Studies* 23 (3): 287–297.

————. 1989. "Skill Reconsidered: The Deskilling and Reskilling of Managers." *Work and Occupations* 16 (1): 65–79.

Reed, Michael. 1985. *Redirections in Organizational Analysis.* London: Tavistock Publications.

Reich, Robert. 1983. *The Next American Frontier.* New York: Times Books.

Reskin, Barbara, and Patricia Roos. 1987. "Status Hierarchies and Sex Segregation." Pp. 3–21 in Christine Bose and Glenna Spitze, eds. *Ingredients for Women's Employment Policy.* Albany: SUNY Press.

Restructuring Turnaround: Experiences in Corporate Renewal. 1987. Business International Research Report. Business International, 12–14, Chemin Riew, CH-1211, Geneva 17, Switzerland.

Roethlisberger, Fritz. 1945. "The Foreman: Master and Victim of Double Talk." *Harvard Business Review* 23 (3): 283–298.

Rosenbaum, James. 1979. "Organizational Career Mobility: Promotion Changes in a Corporation During Periods of Growth and Contraction." *American Journal of Sociology* 85 (1): 21–48.

Rothschild, Emma. 1981. "Reagan and the Real America." *New York Review of Books,* 5 February, pp. 12–18.

Roussakis, Emmanuel. 1984. *Commercial Banking in an Era of Deregulation.* New York: Praeger.

Sabel, Charles. 1982. *Work and Politics: The Division of Labor in Industry.* Cambridge: Cambridge University Press.

Salaman, Graeme. 1978. "Towards a Sociology of Organizational Structure." *Sociological Review* 26 (3): 519–554.

Salaman, Graeme, and Kenneth Thompson. 1980. *Control and Ideology in Organizations.* Cambridge, Mass.: MIT Press.

San Francisco Chronicle. 23 March 1987. "PacBell's New Way to Think." Pp. 1, 6.

———. 27 March 1987. "PacBell 'Kroning'—Figures Soar." P. 1.

Schein, Edgar. 1989. "Reassessing the Divine Rights of Managers." *Sloan Management Review* 30 (2): 63–68.

Schlesinger, Leonard, and B. Oshry. 1984. "Quality of Work Life and the Manager: Muddle in the Middle." *Organizational Dynamics* 13 (1): 4–19.

Schwartz, Felice. 1989. "Management Women and the New Facts of Life." *Harvard Business Review* 89 (1): 65–76.

Schwartz, Jim. 1989. "UAW New Directions: Struggle for the Soul of the Union." *The Nation*, 3 July, pp. 8–10.

Scott, John. 1985. *Corporations, Classes and Capitalism*. London: Hutchison.

Sheinkman, Jack. 1985. "Sharing the Cost of Economic Transition: A Labor Perspective." Pp. 187–193 in Betty Lall, ed. *Economic Dislocation and Job Loss*. Ithaca, N.Y.: Cornell University, School of Industrial and Labor Relations.

Sherwood, John. 1988. "Creating Work Culture with Competitive Advantage." *Organizational Dynamics* 16 (3): 4–27.

Shorris, Earl. 1984. *Scenes from Corporate Life: The Politics of Middle Management*. Harmondsworth: Penguin Books.

Silvestri, G., and J. Lukasiewicz. 1985. "Occupational Employment Projections: The 1984–1995 Outlook." *Monthly Labor Review* 108 (11): 42–57.

Simmons, John, and William Mares. 1985. *Working Together*. New York: Alfred Knopf.

Simpson, Ida Harper. 1989. "The Sociology of Work: Where Have the Workers Gone?" *Social Forces* 76 (3): 563–581.

Smith, Vicki. 1983. "The Circular Trap: Women and Part-Time Employment." *Berkeley Journal of Sociology* 28: 1–17.

Starbuck, William. 1965. "Organizational Growth and Development." Pp. 451–533 in James March, ed. *Handbook of Organizations*. Chicago: Rand-McNally.

Staudohar, Paul, and Holly Brown, eds. 1987. *Deindustriali-*

zation and Plant Closure. Lexington, Mass.: D. C. Heath, Lexington Books.

Staw, B., L. Sandelands, and J. Dutton. 1988. "Threat-Rigidity Effects in Organizational Behavior: A Multilevel Analysis." Pp. 95–116 in K. Cameron, R. Sutton, and D. Whetton, eds. *Readings in Organizational Decline.* Cambridge, Mass.: Ballinger Publishing Co.

Stewart, Rosemary. 1976. "To Understand the Manager's Job: Consider Demands, Constraints, Choices." *Organizational Dynamics* 4 (4): 22–32.

Strober, Myra, and Carolyn Arnold. 1987. "The Dynamics of Occupational Segregation Among Bank Tellers." Pp. 107–157 in Clair Brown and Joseph Pechman, eds. *Gender in the Workplace.* Washington, D.C.: Brookings Institution.

"Ten-Year Merger Completion Record." 1987. *Mergers and Acquisitions* 21 (6): 57.

Thackray, John. 1986. "America's Vertical Cutback." *McKinsey Quarterly*, Autumn, pp. 41–52.

Thomas, Robert. 1988. "Technological Choice: Obstacles and Opportunities for Union-Management Consultation on New Technology." Paper presented at the 83rd Annual Meeting of the American Sociological Association, Atlanta, Georgia, August 27, 1988.

Turnstall, W. Brooke. 1986. "The Break-up of the Bell System: A Case Study in Cultural Transformation." *California Management Review* 28 (2): 110–124.

U.S. Bureau of the Census. 1989. *Statistical Abstracts of the United States.* Table no. 642. "Employed Civilians by Occupation, Sex and Race: 1987." Washington, D.C.: U.S. Bureau of the Census.

Useem, Michael. 1989. "Business Restructuring, Management Control, and Corporate Organization." Department of Sociology, Boston University. Unpublished manuscript.

Uttal, Bro. 1983. "The Corporate Culture Vultures." *Fortune*, 17 October, pp. 66–72.

Wall Street Journal. 2 June 1982. "More Managers are Working Part Time." P. 50.

————. 26 October 1984. "Despite the Expansion, Many Companies Trim Their Labor-Force Size." Pp. 1, 26.

————. 29 November 1984. "Many Middle Managers Fight Back as More Firms Trim Work Forces." Pp. 33, 52.

————. 3 December 1985. "Ford's Leaders Push Radical Shift in Culture as Competition Grows." Pp. 1, 26.

————. 13 January 1987. "IBM Dissidents Hope for Increased Support as Work Force Is Cut." Pp. 1, 27.

————. 3 March 1987. "GM Changes Merit Formula, Cuts Pay Pool." P. 2.

————. 8 April 1987. "Cutting Output, IBM Tells Some Workers: Move, Retire or Quit." Pp. 1, 19.

————. 9 April 1987. "UAL Inc. Takeover Talk Is in the Air." P. 6.

————. 4 May 1987. "As Big Firms Continue to Trim Their Staffs, Two-Tier Setup Emerges." Pp. 1, 12.

————. 26 May 1987a. "Stable Cycles of Executive Careers Shattered by Upheaval in Business." P. 31.

————. 26 May 1987b. "GM is Plagued with Drop in Morale as Payrolls are Cut." Pp. 1, 18.

————. 15 June 1989. "UAW Hotly Debates Whether It Is Too Cozy with Car Companies." Pp. 1, A8.

Wallace, Michael, and Joyce Rothschild. 1988. "Deindustrialization and the Restructuring of American Industry." *Research in Politics and Society* 3. Greenwich, Conn.: JAI Press. Special issue.

Walton, Richard, and Paul Lawrence, eds. 1985. *Human Resources Management: Trends and Challenges.* Boston: Harvard Business School Press.

Wells, Donald M. 1987. *Empty Promises: Quality of Working Life Programs and the Labor Movement.* New York: Monthly Review Press.

Whalley, Peter. 1986. "Markets, Managers, and Technical Autonomy." *Theory and Society* 15 (1–2): 223–247.

Whetton, David. 1980. "Sources, Responses, and Effects of Organizational Decline." Pp. 342–374 in John Kimberly and Robert Miles, eds. *The Organizational Life Cycle: Issues in the Creation, Transformation and Decline of Organizations.* San Francisco: Jossey-Bass.

————. 1988. "Organizational Growth and Decline Processes." Pp. 27–44 in K. Cameron, R. Sutton, and D. Whetton, eds. *Readings in Organizational Decline.* Cambridge, Mass.: Ballinger Publishing Co.

Whyte, William Foote. 1987. "The Employee Ownership Alternative." Pp. 217–226 in Paul Staudohar and Holly Brown, eds. *Deindustrialization and Plant Closure.* Lexington, Mass.: D. C. Heath, Lexington Books.

Whyte, William H. 1956. *The Organization Man.* New York: Simon & Schuster.

Wilkins, Alan. 1989. *Developing Corporate Character: How to Successfully Change an Organization Without Destroying It.* San Francisco: Jossey-Bass.

Willis, Rod. 1987. "What's Happening to America's Middle Managers?" *Management Review* 76 (1): 24–33.

Wishard, Betty. 1985. "Merger: The Human Dimension." *Magazine of Bank Administration* 61 (6): 70–74.

Wood, Stephen. 1982. *The Degradation of Work? Skill, Deskilling and the Labour Process.* London: Hutchison.

Wood, Stephen, ed. 1989. *The Transformation of Work? Skill, Flexibility and the Labour Process.* London: Unwin Hyman.

Work in America. 1973. Report of a Special Task Force to the Secretary of Health, Education and Welfare. Cambridge, Mass.: MIT Press.

Wray, Donald. 1949. "Marginal Men of Industry: The Foremen." *American Journal of Sociology* 54 (4): 298–301.

Wright, Erik, and Bill Martin. 1987. "The Transformation of the American Class Structure, 1960–1980." *American Journal of Sociology* 93 (1): 1–29.

Zeitlin, Maurice. 1974. "Corporate Ownership and Control." *American Journal of Sociology* 79 (5): 1073–1119.

Zimbalist, Andrew, ed. 1979. *Case Studies on the Labor Process.* New York: Monthly Review Press.

Zipp, John, and Katherine Lane. 1987. "Plant Closings and

Control over the Workplace: A Case Study." *Work and Occupations* 14 (1): 62–87.

Zuboff, Shoshanna. 1985. "Technologies That Informate: Implications for Human Resource Management in the Computerized Industrial Workplace." Pp. 103–139 in Richard Walton and Paul Lawrence, eds. *Human Resources Management: Trends and Challenges.* Boston: Harvard Business School Press.

———. 1988. *In the Age of the Smart Machine: The Future of Work and Power.* New York: Basic Books.

Index

Compositor:	Vail-Ballou Press, Inc.
Text:	10/13 Aster
Display:	Helvetica Condensed & Aster
Printer:	Vail-Ballou Press, Inc.
Binder:	Vail-Ballou Press, Inc.